Bible Prophecy Revealed: Book 2

The Beast

and

False Prophet

REVEALED

Revised 2020

D1603290

Michael D. Fortner

Trumpet Press, Lawton, OK

All underlining within quoted material and Scripture is by the author unless otherwise stated.

All scripture verses are from the Holy Bible, New International Version, unless otherwise noted. Copyright © 1973, 1978, 1984, International Bible Society. Used by permission.

Abbreviations & Volumes Used:

BBE – Bible in Basic English
GNB — Good News Bible
KJV – King James Version
LIT – Green's Literal Translation, or The Literal Translation
MEV – Modern English Version (based on the Textus Receptus)
NKJV – New King James Version
NAS – New American Standard
NIV – New International Version
YLT - Young's Literal Translation
CWD – Complete Word Study Dictionary: New Testament,
LXXE – Septuagint, English Translation of the Greek translation of the Old Testament
Strong's numbering is in parentheses ( ) when discussing Greek words.

Library of Congress Catalog-in-Publication Data: 2013930119

Author: Fortner, Michael D.
Title: The Beast and False Prophet Revealed
1. Beast of Revelation 2. Bible Prophecy 3. Book of Revelation 4. Book of Daniel 5. Antichrist

ISBN: 978-0615967349

Trumpet Press is a member of the Christian Indie Publishers Association (CIPA). Visit the author's website for updated info on this book, and sample chapters from his other books: www.usbibleprophecy.com, or michaelfortner.com.

Table of Contents

5

Bible Prophecy Revealed: Book One
Discoveries in Bible Prophecy

Bible Prophecy Revealed: Book Two
The Beast and False Prophet Revealed

Bible Prophecy Revealed: Book Three
The FALL of Babylon the Great America

Bible Prophecy Revealed: Book Four
The Approaching Apocalypse and Three Days of Darkness

Editing God: Textual Criticism and Modern Bibles Analyzed

Satan's False Prophets Exposed

A Note From the Author

You will notice that in this book there are no "end notes" at the end of the chapter or the end of the book. The reason there are no end notes is because it is very troublesome for a reader to lookup a note which may have some important information that will go unread or may only be "Ibid." It is especially difficult to have end notes with an eBook; therefore, this book has been formatted exactly as the eBook version, with notes in the text.

Even though I use the NIV as the main translation in this book, I frequently give a verse in the KJV or Green's Literal Translation (LIT) or some other version because a particular verse may be much more clear in meaning in another translation. Sometimes it takes reading a verse in several translations to see clearly what it actually means in the original Greek.

Also, all underlining in this book is my own, and is never found in the original quotes.

I cite references and tell you where I get information and interpretation; otherwise, you can assume that the interpretation is my own; about 99% of this book is my own interpretation. Even when I quote others, I often will make observations related to the quote which are not found in the original information.

Now a word about quotes. Because of the misuse of source material in other books, from science to religion, some people will suspect that I have taken passages out of context or that I have misrepresented what the prophecy actually says, so I include the actual quotes so you can read them for yourself, at least most of the time. And it is important that you read the quotes to get the most out of this book; I assume that you will read the Scripture passages.

Also, I believe the reader will get the most out of this book by reading it slowly and underling many sentences, because it is very easy to misread critically important statements. I even do some underlining for you.

Should it ever become illegal to criticize Islam in the U.S., this book will be forced to go out of print, but at that time you can freely copy and share the eBook edition of this book for as long as it is illegal. If you live now in a country where it is illegal to criticize Islam, you can now share the eBook edition of this book in that nation.

About the Author

Michael D. Fortner is a journalist (B.A.) and historian with a God-given ability to figure things out and to think outside the box. He is the author of *Discoveries in Bible Prophecy, The Fall of Babylon the Great America, The Approaching Apocalypse and Three Days of Darkness, Satan's False Prophets Exposed,* and *Editing God: Textual Criticism and Modern Bibles Analyzed.*

Introduction

This is the second book of a series of books that takes a new look at Bible prophecy and presents strong evidence that the coming beast and false prophet of the book of Revelation are based solidly in Islam and Muhammad. You will get the most out of this book if you have read the first one, titled *Discoveries in Bible Prophecy*, but it is not required. It is time to open your eyes to the truth about an ancient evil that is reawakening in the Middle East, and now also in Europe!

The Ottoman Empire, the last Islamic empire, will rise from the Abyss as the Scarlet Beast (Rev. 17) to wage jihad upon the world. Islam has encoded in its teachings— murder, lying, plunder, slavery, rape, warfare, and even terrorism as part of its official religious doctrine. Jesus said that the thief comes only to steal, kill, and destroy, and this is exactly what Islam has done from its beginning. Nothing else so completely fits the description in the Bible of the beast and false prophet than Islam, which is more than a religion, but is a totalitarian political system that wants to control every area of your life.

Islam is different from all the other religions that do not believe in Jesus, because Islam officially declares that Jesus is not the Son of God (Quran 4:171; 18:4-5), which is the Biblical definition of Antichrist: *"Who is the liar but he who denies that Jesus is the Christ? This is the Antichrist, he who denies the Father and the Son"* (1 John 2:22).

The spread of Islam has left a trail of blood, suffering, and destruction like no other ideology in world history. History, and even this present age, shows us that Islam is a very violent and fascist religion, full of hate for Christians and Jews. No one could invent a more evil cult.

Islam ruled the second largest empire in history that stretched from the Atlantic Ocean to the borders of China. For over a thousand years the sword of Islam's armies never stopped dripping blood and enslaving the survivors. Millions of Christians have already suffered and died under Islam's armies of conquest, and Christians are still dying today in Egypt, Libya, Iraq, Syria, Nigeria, Sudan, and many other places.

Slavery continued throughout the Muslim invasions and beyond. For hundreds of years the Muslims of North Africa captured European ships, and then American ships, and enslaved the crews. They even raided coastal towns and dragged people out of churches and into slavery where they were beaten and abused in order to pressure them to convert to Islam.

Do not be fooled. The plan to conquer the world and slaughter the Christians and Jews is not a secret conspiracy of the Illuminati or Freemasons! It is broadcast daily on TV, radio, the internet, and in print, and already has almost 2 billion followers.

The beast of Revelation is ready to rise to power. It tried to conquer the world before and will try again. But it will only succeed at bringing World War 3, nuclear war, and global destruction. It will not rule the entire planet, because the "whole world" of the Bible is the Middle Eastern / Mediterranean world, which includes much of Europe. The beast is right now clawing at the edges of the Abyss trying to get out. Even though ISIS is officially defeated, they could still rise again, and even if they don't other organizations are ready to replace them.

There are many other good books that detail the teachings of Islam and the Muslim Brotherhood, but the purpose of this book is to prove that the beast and false prophet will not come out of the European Union, as often taught, but are in fact based in Islam and Islamic empire. I show this by presenting the history of Islam and what the Bible says about it. For example, Muslims call the verses of the Quran, *"miraculous signs."* Revelation 13 tells us that the second beast deceives people with its *"miraculous signs."*

Imams throughout the Islamic world preach that America, Britain, and Israel must be destroyed, and fill their followers with lies about us, saying that all the world's wars and problems are caused by America, Britain, Israel, and democracy. They pray over loudspeakers for Allah to destroy us, calling the people to rise up against us all, but especially America and Israel.

In 2006 a Dutch cartoonist drew a cartoon of Muhammad wearing a turban-bomb to make a political statement against suicide bombers. The reaction was global; Muslims were screaming in the streets. They yelled threats of death while holding signs with threatening messages. People were killed in the demonstrations and riots, and several Christians were murdered by Muslims in retaliation for the cartoon. The demonstrators were not members of Al-Qaeda, but ordinary followers of the religion of peace! The cartoonist now lives under armed guard and moves from place to place because of the threats to his life.

This is the nature and character of Islam.

The riots were repeated in 2012 because of a movie about Muhammad that was made by an Egyptian living in America. The extreme rage is designed to make it illegal to criticize Islam or Muhammad, which will make criminals of all Christians who teach the truth about Islam and the correct interpretation of Bible prophecy. It is already illegal in the UK to say that Islam is not a religion of peace! The two beasts of Revelation 13 do not want their identity revealed.

Even though Egypt has currently outlawed the Muslim Brotherhood, the group is still strong throughout the Muslim world, and will likely be part of the next Islamic empire. In 2010, Mohamed Morsi, who was then the Muslim Brotherhood president of Egypt, said:

> Dear brothers, we must not forget to nurse our children and grandchildren on hatred towards those Zionists and Jews, and all those who support them. They must be nursed on hatred. The hatred must continue. (youtu.be /RCop-dzv29 WY MemriTV)

Islamic clerics have issued rulings that say it is acceptable for the fighters in Syria to rape non-Sunni and non-Muslim (Christian and Jewish) women. But so many women have fled that there are not enough women to rape, so they are recruiting young Muslim women to go there and provide sex to the fighters. It is call *"sex jihad."* (www.raymondibrahim.com/from-the-arab -world/sex-jihad-fatwa-permits-incest-in-syria/   www.humanevents. com/2013/04/02/islamic-cleric-rape-of-non-muslim-syrian-women-permitted/)

Islam does not have any good rules of morality like, *you shalt not kill*, or *love your neighbor as yourself.* But it does teach that you can steal from non-believers, and even enslave and murder them, as we will see in this book.

For several years I thought I was the only one who saw that the beast of Revelation is based in Islam and that another Islamic empire will rise, but I have learned of a few other people who also see it. Here is a quote from *The Rise of the Islamic Empire and the Threat to the West*, by Anthony Dennis:

In short, the coming Islamic Empire will be a world power in every sense of the word, whose people will share a vibrant religion and a common Islamic culture. Like its Muslim predecessors, the Islamic Empire of the early 21st Century will also have an appetite for territorial expansion and military conquest. A modern, worldwide jihad against non-Muslim populations and societies complete with nuclear weapons promises to bring the highest casualty rates in the history of mankind. World War III, if it does come, will probably occur between the Islamic Bloc and the Western nations. It will be the deadliest war ever fought by humanity. (Wyndham Hall Press, 2001, p. 89)

A few others also teach that the beast is based in Islam, but they do not have the details correct. For example, Walid Shoebat believes that the beast is based in Islam until he becomes the Antichrist, but that is not really being based in Islam. No, the beast-empire has literal Islam as its religion; Islam is not just where the beast and false prophet come FROM. And Shoebat's new theory about the mark of the beast is proven wrong in this book.

I also debunk the idea that the mark of the beast is a global account number. I present evidence that 666 is symbolic and points to Islam. For example, Muslims worship on the 6th day of the week, believe in 6 articles of faith, and have 6 volumes of the sayings of Muhammad called the Hadith. But there could also be a literal mark within the revived Islamic empire, such as Muhammad's seal.

I present historical and present-day evidence, but also Scriptural evidence, which proves beyond any doubt that Biblical prophecies of the beast and false prophet, point directly to Islam and its armies of conquest. In short, the seven heads of the beast represent empires that have ruled around the Mediterranean Sea. The head, or empire, that had the fatal wound will rise again. It will not be the Roman Empire, but the last Islamic empire.

The Ottoman Empire was wounded in the 1800s but given the fatal blow during World War I. The nation of Turkey was formed from what was left of the Ottoman Empire. It will rise to become the final head of the beast.

My expository method of interpreting Bible prophecy reveals

many surprising and important insights never before seen. We will learn that the famous *mark of the beast* is NOT the mark of the first beast, but of the *second beast* with two horns. Then there is the surprising revelation about the image of the beast that will shock you, and it is not artificial intelligence!

The visions of Daniel also point to Islam, but most of them were included in Book 1 (BK1). I only have a little of Daniel in this book.

Chapter 1
The Beast of Empire

(1) The True Identity of the Beast

> 1 And the dragon stood on the shore of the sea. And I saw a beast coming out of the sea. He had ten horns and seven heads, with ten crowns on his horns, and on each head a blasphemous name. 2 The beast I saw resembled a <u>leopard</u>, but had feet like those of a <u>bear</u> and a mouth like that of a <u>lion</u>. The dragon gave the beast his power and his throne and great authority. (Revelation 13:1-2)

In order to understand this beast it is first necessary to understand what beasts represent in the Bible. For this we go to Daniel chapter 7 where Daniel saw a vision in which four beasts came up out of the sea. After Daniel describes what he saw, he asked an angel to explain it to him. The angel said:

> 'The four great beasts are four kingdoms that will rise from the earth.' (Dan. 7:17)

It is evident that the beasts represent great military / political kingdoms that will come upon the world, what we call empires. The first beast Daniel saw was like a lion, the second beast like a bear, the third beast like a leopard, the fourth had large iron teeth and ten horns. The beast of Revelation 13 is similar to all four beasts in that it is part lion, part bear, part leopard, and has ten horns. Therefore, the beast of Rev. 13 will be a large and powerful empire.

Empires have the power to do the most harm to the largest number of people, especially God's people, which is why they are seen as vicious beasts in the Bible. Therefore, the beast of

Rev. 13 is <u>not</u> an individual man, called the Antichrist, the final beast is another empire that will rise to power in the Middle East. However, an individual will be leading the empire beast who I refer to as the final Antichrist, since there have been many Antichrists. The Apostle John said the spirit of Antichrist was already in the world during the first century (1 John 4:3).

(2) The Seven Heads of The Beast

Revelation 17 gives us more details about the seven heads:

> 9 "This calls for a mind with wisdom. The seven heads are <u>seven hills</u> on which the woman sits. 10 They are also seven kings. Five have fallen, one is, the other has not yet come; but when he does come, he must remain for a little while. (Rev. 17:9-10)

Even though it says wisdom is needed to figure out the meaning, people quickly jump to the most obvious conclusion, which is not the correct answer. The seven heads of the beast do *not* represent seven of Rome's emperors; the seven heads represent empires that have ruled over the Middle East and Europe during the course of history. One of the empires will rise again, which we will learn about in the following pages.

The text says the seven heads have a double meaning; they represent seven mountains and seven kings. The fact that five kings are fallen and one is not yet come, tells us that the kings rule in succession; one after the other. The passage does *not* mean that five had fallen at the time that John saw this vision. This is one of the reasons why it takes wisdom to understand the meaning.

Notice that the past tense is also used in Rev. 7:14, "*these are those that <u>came out of</u> the Great Tribulation.*" Are we to believe that the Great Tribulation had already taken place when John wrote Revelation? No, likewise, this passage does not refer to five fallen emperors or even five fallen empires by the first century. Five being fallen merely brings us to the time of the 6th head, which is the head that will rise again.

If the seven heads referred to Roman Emperors of the first century, it would require that Revelation be written in 68 A.D.

The five fallen emperors are supposed to be Augustus, Tiberius, Caligula, Claudius, and Nero who committed suicide in 68. The next emperor only ruled a few months, as did the next, both in 68. John wrote Revelation in about 96 A.D., during the rule of Domitian, who was the fourteenth emperor. Those who say it refers to Roman emperors ignore the ones who ruled only a few months, because if they count those that ruled a short time, then it messes everything up. Even though the Bible clearly states that one of the heads will rule only a short time, but the short-reigning rulers are skipped over.

All the previous heads/empires of the beast ruled near or bordered the Mediterranean Sea, especially over Asia Minor and Israel. Even though Israel was not an official nation for almost 1900 years, there were Jews still living in the land, and it was still God's land and his holy city Jerusalem. As far as the Bible is concerned, Jerusalem is the center of the world, which is why the majority of Bible prophecy deals with that part of the world.

If we count all the individual ruling bodies that have existed in that part of the world, there are way more than seven: Egypt, Assyria, Babylon, Media-Persia, Greece, Rome, several Arabic caliphates, Seljuk Turk, Crusader kingdoms, Kingdom of Saladin, Mongol, Ottoman Turk, British, and even more. Often more than one ruled at the same time, side by side, some with many ruling dynasties, and others that were short -lived kingdoms. So what is the answer? First, I believe to be counted as one of the heads they must have ruled over the land of Israel because Israel is the main focus of the Bible.

The Mongols did not rule Palestine or even Syria, so they did not conquer far enough into the region to be counted; likewise the U.S.S.R. did not rule within the Middle East. The Crusader kingdoms were small, mostly encompassing Palestine. But even if you don't count these kingdoms, there are too many.

We can examine it any number of ways, to exclude one empire or another, like counting all the Islamic-based kingdoms as one, but it is still hard to come up with a definitive list that most people can feel are the right kingdoms without raising many objections. In the end I believe the number 7 gives us the answer.

In the Bible, the number 7 appears more than any other number, from Genesis to Revelation, and it carries much symbolic meaning, which boils down to fullness, completeness. Therefore, I believe the 7 heads of the beast are not to be taken as an exact number, but merely represent the total number of empires that have or will rule over the Mediterranean / Middle Eastern world. Perhaps the seven heads represent the last seven empires. The main heads of the beast are: Babylon, Media-Persia, Greece, Rome, Arabic Islamic kingdoms, Ottoman Empire, and the British Empire.

(3) Seventh Head of the Beast

Because there are 7 heads on the beast, many people believe the 7th head of the beast will be the final head, but that is not the case, because Rev. 17 clearly describes an 8th head that has not yet come to power and will be explained shortly. About the 7th head, Rev. 17:10 says, *"but when he does come, he must remain for a little while."*

Since the British Empire was the last empire to rule in that part of the world, and it only ruled there a short time, it must be the 7th head of the beast. The British Empire conquered the Ottoman Empire in WWI and ruled Egypt and the Middle Eastern nations after the war. It remained only a short time because it gradually gave independence to most of its subject nations during the 20th century, thereby ceasing to be a beastly empire (see BK1). At this time there are no empires in any part of the world, in the classical sense. So the beast is currently dead, but will soon come to life again.

Some people may want to argue that the British Empire existed long before it ruled over Egypt, the Middle-East, and Palestine; that is true, but not only did it rule Israel after the Ottoman Empire, it also came into being after the Ottoman Empire came into being and did not last as long as many of the previous heads of the beast.

And it ruled the nations around the Mediterranean and Israel the shortest length of time of all the previous empires. So, it stands to reason that the British Empire is the seventh head that we are told will rule only a short time. Especially since no other empire took its place. The final eighth head of the beast will be one of the former heads, which is why we only see seven heads.

What about the USSR? It came into being in 1917 and only lasted about 74 years; wouldn't it be the seventh head of the beast? It cannot be one of the heads of the beast for the simple reason that it never ruled over the nation of Israel and never ruled over any Middle Eastern /Mediterranean or Western European nations. Though Satan has had many empires in history, they are not shown to us in Revelation, because the main focus of Rev. is the Middle Eastern/Mediterranean/European region.

Even though the beast will be among the nations that burn America with fire during WW3, this beast will not be able to conquer and rule over the U.S.A. for centuries the way they conquered and ruled the Christians of the Eastern Roman Empire, from Egypt to the Balkans. Which is why many Christians have historically been, *"out of the serpent's reach"* (Revelation 12:14, see Bk1 for a full discussion of this passage).

(4) The Final Eighth Head of the Beast

The next question becomes, what about the next head of the beast? Rev. 17, which will be discussed shortly, says the beast actually has eight heads, not seven, but it only shows seven because the eighth will be one of the previous seven, revived. All the nations that Assyria, Babylon, and Media-Persia ruled over are today Islamic. The same is true of the Ottoman Empire, which was the 6th head.

The nation of Greece is not Islamic, but Greece is today very weak, and barely able to survive as a nation because of extreme economic problems. Even though the four generals who ruled Alexander's empire were Greek, if you look at a map of all four kingdoms, today those kingdoms are 90% Islamic.

The Roman Empire converted to Christianity in the fourth century and was so large it became divided with two capitals; the city of Rome was the western capital, and Constantinople the eastern. When the Roman Empire supposedly fell, it was actually only part of the western half that fell; the eastern capital continued to rule most of the empire but is referred to by historians as the Byzantine Empire even though it was officially known as the Roman Empire. I refer to it in this book as the Eastern Roman Empire.

("Byzantine" was a term sometimes used to refer to the Eastern Romans because of Constantinople's heritage, like the original British and first Americans are known as Anglo-Saxons because of their heritage. And even in the Bible, the Babylonians are called *Chaldeans*, which is what they were in past centuries.)

The Eastern Roman Empire successfully held back the barbarians, even the Vikings were held back. It ruled the regions of Egypt, Palestine, Iraq, Syria, Greece, Bulgaria, Albania, Bosnia, Croatia, many islands of the Mediterranean, Asia Minor (Turkey), and part of North Africa. For a time it even ruled most of Italy after the fall of the city of Rome.

The Eastern Roman Empire maintained the Justinian laws which became the basis for the laws of most European nations.

> [The Eastern Roman Empire] supervised education and maintained hospitals and asylums for the old, the orphaned, the sick, and the destitute, and imperial legislation as a whole reflected the constant concern of the emperor for the welfare of his subjects. (*Funk & Wagnalls New Encyclo.*, V.4, p.421)

With up to a million inhabitants, Constantinople was the largest and richest city during the Middle Ages and was a major center of trade. But the Eastern Roman Empire was gradually conquered by the Muslims over a period of more than 800 years.

The final Islamic empire was the Ottoman Empire that was only defeated in WW I, only a little more than 100 years ago, so if one of the former heads of the beast is going to rise again, the Ottoman Empire is the best candidate.

I explained in Book 1 that Revelation chapter 9 tells us that 4 angels bound at the Euphrates River will be released to kill 1/3rd of mankind. The Euphrates River begins in Turkey and flows through Syria, then through Iraq. Therefore, this tells us for a fact that WW3 will begin in this region, or is at least caused by the people that live in this region. So if we are talking about a revived empire that is going to wage war with a ~~desire to destroy Jews and Christians~~, then the final head of the beast can only be a revived ~~Islamic empire,~~ most likely Ottoman.

The reason it cannot be a revived British Empire is because if Britain had any interest in having an empire it would not have willingly given independence to most of its subject nations (except Northern Ireland). It is also not trying to reconstitute its empire. But most importantly, it was not killed in warfare like the Ottoman and Babylonian beast-empires were killed, Britain gave up its empire willingly.

(5) A War Against the Saints

All previous heads of the beast made war upon God's righteous to various degrees, but the final head of the beast will be worse than all the previous heads, even worse than the Ottoman Empire. The main purpose of the beast is to engage in a war, as we are told twice in Rev. 13.

> Men worshiped the dragon because he had given authority to the beast, and they also worshiped the beast and asked, "Who is like the beast? Who can <u>make war</u> against him?" (Rev. 13:4)

The second reference in verse 7 clearly states that it will be a war against Christians:

> He was given power to <u>make war against the saints</u> and to conquer them. (Rev. 13:7)

Islam governs every area of life: political, and social. It demands to rule the world politically even more than it desires to spread its religion, which is why the Muslim armies of the past required people who did not want to convert to Islam to at least submit to Islamic rule. Islam openly declares that it must rule the whole world and is calling all Muslims to join together in a global Holy War to accomplish that goal.

Here is a quote from a Friday sermon given by Sheik Ibrahim Mudeiris that was broadcast on Palestinian Authority TV:

Allah has tormented us with "the people most hostile to the believers" – the Jews. "Thou shalt find that the people most hostile to the believers to be the Jews and the polytheists [Christians]." Allah warned His beloved Prophet Muhammad about the Jews, who had killed their prophets, forged their Torah, and sowed corruption throughout their history.

With the establishment of the state of Israel, the entire Islamic nation was lost, because Israel is a cancer spreading through the body of the Islamic nation, and because the Jews are a virus resembling AIDS, from which the entire world suffers. You will find that the Jews were behind all the civil strife in this world. The Jews are behind the suffering of the nations.

. . . We have ruled the world before, and by Allah, the day will come when we will rule the entire world again. The day will come when we will rule America. The day will come when we will rule Britain and the entire world – except for the Jews. The Jews will not enjoy a life of tranquility under our rule, because they are treacherous by nature, as they have been throughout history. The day will come when everything will be relieved of the Jews - even the stones and trees which were harmed by them. Listen to the Prophet Muhammad, who tells you about the evil end that awaits Jews. The stones and trees will want the Muslims to finish off every Jew. (5.13.2005) (www.israpundit.com/archives/2005/05/sheik_Ibrahim_mphp)

Those are proud and boastful words, which accurately describe Muhammad and his followers, and it agrees with what it says in Revelation 13 about the Islamic beast:

The beast was given a mouth to utter proud words and blasphemies and to exercise his authority for forty-two months. 6 He opened his mouth to blaspheme God, and to slander his name and his dwelling place and those who live in heaven. (Rev. 13:5-6)

Muslims have been speaking and acting against Jehovah (Yahweh) and Jews and Christians for 1400 years. No one in the world hates the Jews and Christians more than Muslims. Today, the hate of Muslims seems to be increasing as Christians around the world are being killed in ever-increasing numbers; Churches are being burned, homes are being burned, and it will only get worse. According to many sources, a Christian in the Middle East is murdered every five minutes, but <u>that was before the start of the *Arab Spring*</u>. You rarely hear about that on American news; they only like to broadcast when a Palestinian is killed while rioting, and blame the Jews.

Muslims all speak proudly and boastfully because that is the way Muhammad spoke, and how he wrote in the Quran. Islam even claims that the passages in the Bible that refer to the coming of the Holy Spirit, the Comforter, actually refer to Muhammad; this is blasphemy. Muslims may as well stand up and declare that they are the followers of Antichrist.

It is a bit ironic that the Muslims are the followers of Antichrist, yet they see themselves as punishers of evil doers, the arm of God's wrath upon the wicked, which is partly correct. God told the Israelites that if they repented they would not be destroyed, but if they did not, the armies of Babylon would come and carry out God's wrath upon them. They did not repent and were destroyed by the Babylonians. God used pagans to punish his chosen people. A similar thing happened with the Muslims against the Christians of the Eastern Roman Empire, and will happen again.

The Christians of the 7th and 8th centuries had a crisis of faith and questioned God about why he allowed the Muslims to devastate them. They believed that the coming of the Muslims was in fact a judgment from God because of their sins and false doctrines. Many of the eastern Christians believed in monophysitism, which is the belief that Christ did not have two natures, human and divine, but only one nature, divine. Some even said the destruction was because of worshiping icons, and icon veneration was banned for many years in the 8th century, but eventually brought back. In the near future, God will once again allow the rise of bloodthirsty Islamic armies to punish the lukewarm, compromised, and money-loving Christians of Europe and America. Revelation 13 continues:

> 7 He was given power to <u>make war against the saints</u> and to conquer them. And he was given authority over every tribe, people, language and nation. 8 All inhabitants of the earth will worship the beast-- <u>all whose names have not been written in the book of life</u> belonging to the Lamb that was slain from the creation of the world. (Rev. 13:7-8)

Notice that it <u>does *not* say that all people will worship the beast</u>; it says all will worship <u>who are not Christians</u>. It says the beast will "*make war*" against Christians, which is what the Arabs and Turks did, and are doing right now. The next Muslim empire will continue the same war against Christians as it attacks them within Muslim nations and invades countries where they live.

The Gospel has spread so much in Africa that a few nations have majority Christian populations, so they too are in danger of being invaded. The next passage in Rev. 13 clearly describes the coming war against Christians:

> He who has an ear, let him hear. 10 If anyone is to go into captivity, into captivity he will go. If anyone is to be killed with the sword, with the sword he will be killed. This calls for patient endurance and faithfulness on the part of the saints. (Rev. 13:9-10)

Politicalislam.com estimates that 270 million people were killed in 1400 years of jihad and Islamic rule. I think that number is conservative. Even more have suffered slavery or persecution because of Islam. Sadly, these events will be replayed.

Notice that it does not say that only sinners or sinful Christians will go into captivity or be killed. It does not say the righteous will escape captivity or escape being killed. The prophet Daniel was taken into captivity by Babylon during one of its invasions of Israel.

But this time the beast will not have long to do its evil. Christians should wait patiently knowing that God will destroy the beast. It will only last 42 months because God will stop it by the 7th Bowl of Wrath of Rev. 16 that will destroy the beast and false prophet, but most of the world will also be destroyed, which is described in detail in Book 4. The destruction of America is described in detail in Book 3.

Chapter 2
The Quran and Hadith

Many Muslims try to claim that Islam is a religion of peace, but anyone who studies both the Quran and history, knows that Islam is anything but a religion of peace. Islam's holy book says:

> We shall cast terror into the hearts of those who disbelieve, because they joined others in worship with Allâh . . . (Quran 3:151) (Translation is *The Noble Quran*.)

This verse refers to attacking Christians because they believe in the Trinity. One of the Quran's primary verses tells people "*to fight in Allah's way, so they slay and are slain.*" Is it a mere coincidence that this chapter and verse is (9:111)? There are a lot of these "coincidences" that point to the evil of Islam, so many that it is hard to believe that they are just coincidences. Muhammad said:

> And warn those who say: Allah has taken a son. They have no knowledge of it, nor had their fathers; a grievous word it is that comes out of their mouths; they speak nothing but a lie. (Quran 18:4-5) (Shakir translation)

That quote is surely blasphemy. Another verse is engraved in gold leaf around the inside of the Dome of the Rock:

> "O followers of the Book [Bible], do not exceed the limits in your religion, and do not speak (lies) against Allah, but (speak) the truth; the Messiah, Jesus son of Mary, is only an apostle of Allah . . . Far be it from His glory that He should have a son . . ." (Quran 4:171) (Shakir)

Murder and slavery became a fundamental part of Islam when Muhammad slaughtered the male members of an opposing tribe and sold the women and children into slavery. It is even in the Islamic holy books, the Quran and Hadith:

> . . . bring them with chains on their necks till they embrace Islam. (Hadith: Vol. 6, Book 60, # 80: Narrated Abu Huraira)

Slavery continued throughout the Muslim invasions and beyond. Dr. Bill Warner is the founder of the *Center for the Study of Political Islam* (CSPI). He relates this story about Khalid, one of the great generals and companions of Muhammad:

> Mohammed sent Khalid out, and the sword of Allah to the Jazima tribe to offer Islam, they refused. He annihilated every one of them. At the battle of Olayis in Iraq, for two days he spent out rounding up the losers, put them in a dry stream bed and cut off their heads until the stream ran with blood. He then took the captain of the Zoroastrian Persian tribe, his wife was there. He cut off the man's head, let the blood drain into the soil and raped his wife in the bloody soil.

> That was one of the companions of Mohammed. This is the nature of jihad. Where did Khalid learn how to do that? From Mohammed. From Mohammed at the Battle of Khaybar. (*Why We are Afraid, a 1400 year Secret*, politicalislam.com, also at: www.youtube.com/watch?v=t_Qpy0mXg8Y)

According to several sources, Khalid ordered his men to murder everyone they found when they entered Damascus, because the city did not willingly surrender:

> "No quarter to the enemies of Allah," yelled Khalid, known as the Sword of Allah. He was a mass murderer, robber, and slaver of Christians. . . . his trumpets sounded, and a torrent of Christian blood was poured down the streets of Damascus. (*The Decline and Fall of the Roman Empire*, by Edward Gibbon.)

A quote from a little book intended only for English speaking Muslims, and published in Saudi Arabia, details the life of a man named *Saad bin Abi Waqqas* who has gone down in Islamic history with great honor because "*he was the first Muslim who had the honour to shed* [the] *blood of unbelievers*" (*Saad bin Abi Waqqas,* by Aamaal Khattab, 1999, p. 9).

Again the Quran says:

> Fight against those who believe not in Allah, nor in the Last
> Day, nor forbid that which has been forbidden by Allah and His
> Messenger and those who acknowledge not the religion of truth
> (Islam) among the people of the Scripture (Jews and Christians),
> until they pay the Jizyah (tax on non-believers) with willing sub-
> mission, and feel themselves subdued. (*Noble Quran* 9:29)

The Shakir translation says, *"until they pay the tax in acknowl-
edgment of superiority and they are in a state of subjection."* In other
words, fight until Islam rules the world politically and nonMuslims pay a heavy tax and are oppressed under Islamic rule. Muslim rulers have always oppressed Christians and Jews by discriminatory laws. Another verse suggests that Muslims must
wage war until there is no other religion:

> And slay them wherever you find them . . . for persecution is
> worse than slaughter . . . And fight them until persecution is no
> more, and religion is for Allah. (Quran 2:191, 193) (Pickthal
> translation)

In other words, it is better to "slaughter" people in order to
conquer them than be in subjection to them. The first Muslim
war of conquest began in 632 and succeeded beyond their wild-
est expectations. When the Muslim general, Akbah, reached the
Atlantic Ocean, it is reported that—

> He spurred his horse into the waves, and, raising his eyes to
> heaven, exclaimed with the tone of a fanatic, "Great God! if my
> course were not stopped by this sea, I would still go on, to the
> unknown kingdoms of the West, preaching the unity of thy holy
> name, and putting to the sword the rebellious nations who wor-
> ship any other gods than thee." (*The Rise and Fall of the Roman
> Empire*, by Edward Gibbon)

The ocean stopped the Muslim advance at that time, but they
still desire to continue their jihad to the ends of the Earth, and
will try again.

Ishmael is one of the ancestors of the Arabs. He was the son
of Abraham and Hagar, his concubine. The Bible says Ishmael
will live like a wild man and will be against everyone and everyone will be against him (Gen. 16:12), and that very aptly de-

scribes Muslims; many have the DNA of Ishmael but they all have that spirit that wants to fight and kill anyone for the slightest reason.

One of Allah's 99 names is the Great Deceiver. Muhammad said:

Allah is the greatest of all deceivers. (Quran 3.54)

The Apostle John said:

I say this because many deceivers, who do not acknowledge Jesus Christ as coming in the flesh, have gone out into the world. Any such person is the deceiver and the antichrist. (2 John 1:7)

Muhammad said:

The Hour [Day of Judgment] will not be established until you fight with the Jews, and the stone behind which a Jew will be hiding will say. "O Muslim! There is a Jew hiding behind me, so kill him." (Hadith 4:52:177)

Jesus said:

You belong to your father, the devil, and you want to carry out your father's desires. He was a murderer from the beginning, not holding to the truth, for there is no truth in him. When he lies, he speaks his native language, for he is a liar and the father of lies. (John 8:44)

Muhammad said:

And it was not [possible] for this Qur'an to be produced by other than Allah, but [it is] a confirmation of what was before it and a detailed explanation of the [former] Scripture, about which there is no doubt, from the Lord of the worlds. (Quran 10:37)

The Apostle Paul called Satan the god of this world:

The god of this world has blinded the minds of those who do not believe . . . (2 Corinthians 4:4)

The Quran was supposedly given to Muhammad by the angel Gabriel. Muhammad said:

Whoever is an enemy to Gabriel-for he brings down the (revelation) to thy heart by Allah's will, a confirmation of what went before, and guidance and glad tidings for those who believe . . . (Quran 2:97)

The Apostle Paul Said:

> But even if we or an angel from heaven should preach a gospel other than the one we preached to you, let them be under God's curse! (Galatians 1:8)

Muhammad even appears to say that all followers of Islam have a demon assigned to them, and that he also has one!

> There is none amongst you with whom is not an attache from amongst the jinn (devil). They (the Companions) said: Allah's Messenger, with you too? Thereupon he said: Yes, but Allah helps me against him and so I am safe from his hand and he does not command me but for good. (Hadith 39:6757)

He also said:

> The most awful name in Allah's sight on the Day of Resurrection, will be (that of) a man calling himself Malik Al-Amlak (the king of kings). (Hadith 8:73:224)

But Muslims are going to see that sight! Revelation says of Christ:

> The armies in heaven, clothed in fine linen, white and clean, followed Him on white horses. . . . On His robe and on His thigh He has a name written: KING OF KINGS AND LORD OF LORDS. (Rev. 19:14, 16)

Revelation 17:8 describes the coming of the 8th head of the beast as rising up *"out of the Abyss."* Revelation 9 describes the opening of the Abyss, and says locusts came up out of the Abyss:

> They had as king over them the angel of the Abyss, whose name in Hebrew is Abaddon, and in Greek, Apollyon. 12 The first woe is past; two other woes are yet to come. (9:11-12)

Abaddon and Apollon both mean *"the Destroyer,"* therefore, the name of the ruler of this revived empire is *"the Destroyer."* In the Quran, Allah is described using many different names, much the way that Yahweh has many names in the Bible such as El-Shaddai, God Almighty. One of the names of Allah, depending on who does the translation from Arabic, is *"the Destroyer."* I will not include all 99 names, but here is a sampling:

1. Ar-Rahman: The All-Merciful

9. Al-JaKhali: The Creator

15. Al-bbar: The Compeller

11. Al-Qahhar: The Subduer

62. Al-Mumeet: The Creator of Death, The Destroyer, The One who renders the living dead. (www.faizani .com/articles / names. html www. ahadith. co.uk/99 namesof Allah.php?)

Some websites have the names numbered one digit differently and spelled differently; wikipedia.org has it this way:

61. Al-Mumit: The Destroyer, The Bringer of Death . . . (en. wikipedia.org/wiki/Names_of_God_in_Islam)

So this passage in Revelation 9 literally names *Allah* as being the power behind the beast of Revelation! Given the history of what Islam has done to the nations it invaded and conquered, and is still doing today, *"the destroyer"* exactly describes Islam.

In 2 Thessalonians 2, the man of lawlessness comes from what is spiritually dead, which is why he is called, *"son of perdition."* Islam came from paganism, and Muhammad was a pagan before he claimed to follow one god. Historical evidence shows that Allah was the chief deity in Mecca before the coming of Islam and was the god of Muhammad's tribe (www. faith freedom. org/ Articles/ skm30804.htm), and was only one of 360 gods in the Kaaba.

The Greek for "perdition" is *apoleia* (from apollumi), and literally means *"to destroy fully"* (CWD). It can refer to either physical or spiritual destruction and ruin. Notice the closeness in spelling and meaning to *apollyon* (Rev. 9:11), and means *"the Destroyer."* This is because *apollyon* also comes from *apollumi*. So *son of perdition* or "destroyer" points us directly to Islam, because Allah is the Destroyer, as we learned in a previous chapter. So, the passage is saying that the coming Antichrist is the *"son of destruction."*

Although this passage in 2 Thess. could refer to the next global leader of Islam, the final Antichrist, it certainly does refer to Muhammad who founded Islam. Mohammad was the first genuine Antichrist, and the next leader of Islam will be the final Antichrist.

Chapter 3
A Brief History of Islam

(1) The Caliphs

An understanding of the history of Islam and the empires it created is necessary for a full understanding of the coming final beast of Revelation, because it will be a revived Islamic empire.

The word "caliph" literally means successor, and refers to the rulers of Islam after Muhammad. Some of the caliphs in the Arabic Empire were actually related to Muhammad by blood or marriage. There were many different dynasties of caliphs, such as the Umayyads, Fatimids, Abbasids; most had to fight other Muslims to stay in power.

The first four caliphs are called the *Rightly Guided Caliphs* by Sunni Muslims. The first after Muhammad was Abu Bakr (632-634). He died after an illness, and some people suspect he may have been poisoned by a rival group who desired to field the successor. Muhammad had married one of Bakr's daughters. Before his death, Abu Bakr appointed Umar his successor.

Umar (634-644) (also known as Omar), converted to Islam in 616 and was murdered by a Persian slave. He was stabbed in the stomach six or seven times and died three days later. Rather than appoint his successor, he appointed a six-man committee to choose his successor. Muhammad had also married one of his daughters.

The third caliph was Uthman who was murdered in 656 by one or more rebel groups who disagreed with some of his actions. He became caliph at age 65 and was married to two of Muhammad's daughters; when the first died, he married the second.

Ali (656-661) was the cousin of Muhammad and had been the first male to convert to Islam. Ali married Fatima, daughter of Muhammad, whose children were the only grandchildren of Muhammad to survive. Ali became the fourth caliph which brought a civil war among the Muslims, the relatives of Uthman against Ali. Ali won the early battles, then Mu'awiya, the governor of Syria, who was also a relative of Uthman, fought against Ali for the caliphate. Ali was murdered by a relative of someone who was killed in the battles, then Mu'awiya fought against Ali's generals and appointed himself caliph. Mu'awiya then started the Umayyad Dynasty of ruling caliphs by passing the office on to his children, which lasted 661-750. These are called Sunni Muslims, but Shia Muslims consider Ali and his descendants the rightful heirs of the caliphate, which has resulted in much bloodshed over the centuries.

Many of the caliphs from 632-1250 were either murdered or died fighting other Muslims. Rebellions, murders, assassinations, and civil wars were normal among the Muslims. The seat of government was moved to Damascus when Mu'awiya became the 6th caliph, if you count Muhammad as the 1st. The caliphs ruled over the entire empire, but there were regional governors called amirs and sultans. Because the empire grew very large, as time went by some regions began to rule themselves politically, but they were still officially part of the caliphate. Though the caliphs' political power grew weak, they were still seen as religious leaders, so it was still an Islamic empire.

A civil war killed all the Umayyads and thus began the Abbasid Dynasty that ruled 750-1031, but a rival caliphate formed in North Africa called the Fatimid (909-1171) and another in Spain and north-western Africa. Ultimately, the Ottomans conquered the Middle East and Egypt and transferred the caliphate to Istanbul in 1517 where it remained until it was abolished after WWI.

(2) The Invasions

The Arabic Islamic Empire began in 632 A.D. when the followers of Muhammad began their wars of conquest. They invaded Persia and the southern territories of the Eastern Roman Empire, such as Syria. Palestine fell in 637, Egypt in 642, Cyprus in 649, and the remainder of North Africa between 670-698.

When the Muslim armies approached a city they offered the inhabitants three choices:

1. Convert to Islam

2. Submit to Islamic rule and live under oppressive laws and heavy taxes.

3. Be attacked by Muslim armies, and if defeated, suffer death or slavery.

If the city chose to fight and was defeated, it was plundered, the men of fighting age were murdered or sold into slavery, and most of the women and children were raped and sold into slavery. Sometimes the Arabs would slaughter every man, woman, and child in a city that resisted them, just to strike fear into other cities so they would submit. Those who did submit were heavily taxed. Many Christians lost all their possessions, or their lives, to the invading Muslims. Whole regions were depopulated by slaughter or the inhabitants fleeing to other areas. An Egyptian, John of Nikiou, wrote about the atrocities committed there:

> Then the Muslims arrived in Nikiou. There was not one single soldier to resist them. They seized the town and slaughtered everyone they met in the street and in the churches — men, women, and children, sparing nobody. Then they went to other places, pillaged and killed all the inhabitants they found. . . .

> The patriarch Cyrus felt deep grief at the calamities in Egypt, because Amr, who was of barbarian origin, showed no mercy in his treatment of the Egyptians and did not fulfill the covenants which had been agreed with him. . . .

> After taking possession of Alexandria, he had the town's canal drained . . . He raised the tax to as much as twenty-two batr of gold, with the result that the inhabitants, crushed down by the

burden and in no position to pay it, went into hiding. . . .

> But it is impossible to describe the lamentable position of the inhabitants of this town, who came to the point of offering their children in exchange for the enormous sums that they had to pay each month, finding no one to help them because God had abandoned them and had delivered the Christians into the hands of their enemies. (Bostom, *Legacy of Jihad*, page 590)

The writers of the 7th and 8th centuries stated that Christian women were being taken captive and sold into slavery and prostitution (*Seeing Islam as Others Saw It:* by Robert G. Hoyland, p. 98). Thomas the Presbyter wrote about 640 A.D., (but he used a different calendar):

> In the year 945, indiction 7, on Friday, 4 February, (634) at the ninth hour, there was a battle between the Romans and the Arabs of Muhammad (*tayyiiye d-Mhmt*) in Palestine twelve miles east of Gaza. The Romans fled, leaving behind the patriarch *bryrdn* [Syrian, BRYRDN], whom the Arabs killed. Some 4000 poor villagers of Palestine were killed there, Christians, Jews and Samaritans. The Arabs ravaged the whole region. (*Seeing Islam as Others Saw It*, by Robert G. Hoyland, page 120)

These horrible events were repeated in region after region. A Christian Lebanese writer said when the Muslims invaded Lebanon they *"raped their way through the country,"* (Gabriel, *Because They Hate*, page 14).

Armenia, the small Christian country north of Iran, was invaded many times by Muslim armies because the Armenians refused to gradually convert to Islam over the centuries like other Middle East nations did, and they occasionally rebelled against their oppressors. Sebeos the historian describes their first invasion in 642:

> The ravaging army left Assyria and, by way of Dzor, entered the Taron region, which it seized . . . they crossed the bridge, and invaded the whole region. After taking a considerable quantity of booty and captives, they camped at the edge of the forest of Khosrovakert.

> On the fifth day, they launched an attack on the town of Dvin, and it fell to them; for they had shrouded it in clouds of smoke

and, by this means and by arrow shots, they drove back the men who were defending the ramparts. Then, having set up their ladders, they climbed on to the walls, hurled themselves into the square and opened the gates.

The enemy's army rushed in and <u>butchered the inhabitants of the town by the sword</u>. After gorging itself on booty, it returned to its encampments, outside the town.

After a few days' rest, the Ishmaelites went back whence they had come, dragging after them a host of captives, numbering thirty-five thousand. (*Legacy of Jihad*, P. 593. English translation from Bat Ye'or, *The Decline of Eastern Christianity under Islam*, pp. 274-275)

In Africa, Muslims were enslaving large numbers of natives, so entire tribes converted to Islam because believers could not be enslaved; however, conversion after enslavement did not result in freedom but did result in better treatment. In 643 after seven years of siege, the city of Caesarea fell to the Arabs who then slaughtered 7,000 of its citizens. In 650 Cyprus was plundered, and the region of Isauria, *"they put to death many inhabitants and returned to Damascus with 5,000 captives as slaves"* (*Legacy of Jihad*, Bostom, p. 390).

A book written by a Muslim about the Islamic conquests, reveals much shocking truth about Islam and what happened during the wars of conquest, which Muslims refer to as "openings," because it means opening up the country to Islamic rule. The following quote from the book begins with a statement by people who were being attacked, and decided to submit to Islam:

"O you Arabs! Can't you stop your harshness? How can we tell you that we believe you and demand a cessation of fighting and you aim at nothing but fighting?"

Abu 'Ubaidah said, "Yes, because this is more worthy to us than life, for <u>it is the way by which we ask for the pardon and forgiveness of our Lord</u>." (*The Islamic Openings*, by Abdul Aziz Al -Shinnawy, Egypt, 2002, page 163-164)

The only guarantee a Muslim has of entering heaven is if he dies fighting in jihad. The book goes on to reveal the treachery of the Muslims, by not always honoring their agreements:

> Sa'id besieged them till they asked for a treaty of peace and safe-
> ty. He agreed to the condition that he would not kill one of them.
> However, when they opened the fort, he killed them all saving
> one man and took as spoils everything that was there. (Ibid, page
> 270)

The above passage also shows how they will engage in mass murder without a second thought.

Muslims invaded Spain in 711 slaughtering and enslaving; they burned convents and monasteries, raped and beheaded, and even crucified people. France was invaded in 721, and all of Europe was in danger of being overrun, but Charles Martel stopped them at the Battle of Tours (Poitiers) in 732.

A hundred years later they tried to invade Europe again through Italy and actually established coastal bases in several places from which they sacked and burned Italian cities, plundering and burning churches and libraries. Thousands of Christian men, women, and children were killed or taken into slavery in these attacks. Now we can understand why the Europeans felt the Crusades were necessary. No incursions were made into Europe during the time of the Crusades.

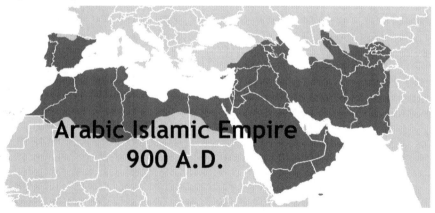

The Muslims today would have you believe that they were welcomed in many areas, and that after the conquests the Christians and Jews lived unmolested as "protected" people under Islamic rulers, but that is far from the truth. There were times when they lived freely, but much of the time the Christians and Jews were badly persecuted and even slaughtered, with churches being destroyed, such as when the Arabs suffered defeats by the Eastern Roman armies, or when the Muslims warred with each other:

> Greek sources of the eighth century speak also of the savagery of Saracen robbers who raided various monasteries, killing and plundering. For example, during the caliphate of Harun al-Rashid (786-809), the monasteries of Palestine suffered from numerous raids. Many monks were put to death. The monastery of St. Sabbas was invaded in 786 and several monks were slaughtered. . . .
>
> . . . Harun al-Rashid issued a decree (797) ordering the destruc-tion of Christian churches; he also imprisoned several bishops. Harun was not an exception; several caliphs were especially in-tolerant toward churches and monasteries. When Marwan II fled before the Abbasid troops, he plundered and destroyed many churches and monasteries in Egypt. . . .
>
> Bar Hebraeus relates that Caliph al-Mahdi (775-785) forcefully converted 5,000 Christians of Aleppo. It was not only the ca-liphs, however, who often resorted to violent means against the hierarchs of the churches. Bar Hebraeus reports that mobs often assailed the Christians whenever the government was weak or reluctant to punish the Christians. . . . Mob action became very frequent in the eighth century. (*Greek Christian and Other Ac-counts of the Muslim Conquests of the Near East*, by Demetrios Con-stantelos, quoted *in Legacy of Jihad* by Bostom, page 392-393, 395)

We can see now just how Islam became the dominate religion throughout the Middle East and North Africa. The Muslims were even more ruthless during the invasions of India. In the 13th century, Balban ruled as Ulugh Khan Khan Khan-i-Azam:

> He made a proclamation that a soldier who brought a live cap-tive would be rewarded with two silver tankahs and one who brought the head of a dead one would get one silver tankah. Soon three or four hundred living and dead were brought to his presence. . . .

The exact figures of such slaves have not been mentioned and therefore cannot be computed. All that is known is that they were captured in droves. (*Muslim Slave System in Medieval India*, by K.S. Lal. Quoted in *Legacy of Jihad*, Bostom, page 542)

(3) Islam and Slavery

Slavery has always been an important part of Islam. Muslims have probably sold more people into slavery than the rest of the world combined:

> The point to note is that [the] taking of slaves was a matter of routine in every expedition. Only when the numbers were exceptionally large did they receive the notice of the chroniclers. So that in Mahmud's attack on Ninduna in the Punjab (1014), Utbi says that "slaves were so plentiful that they became very cheap; and men of respectability in their native land (India) were degraded by becoming slaves of common shop-keepers (in Ghazni)."

> His statement finds confirmation in later chronicles . . . Next year from Thanesar, according to Farishtah, "the Muhammadan army brought to Ghaznin 200,000 captives so that the capital appeared like an Indian city, for every soldier of the army had several slaves and slave girls." (*Muslim Slave System in Medieval India*, by K.S. Lal. Quoted in *Legacy of Jihad*, Bostom, p. 551)

The Ottoman Turks were just as enthusiastic about slavery as the Arabs had been. An eyewitness wrote about it in 15th century:

> Bartholome de Yano paints a gripping picture of their sufferings: "Priests, monks, the young and the aged who could scarcely walk, were shackled and drawn by horses," whereas the able-bodied men were led with the women and children like a flock being guarded by dogs. "Those who lingered along the way because of weariness, thirst, or rather their sufferings, were killed on the spot." Others succumbed to their illnesses. Bartholome de Yano saw in the streets of Adrianople heaps of corpses partially devoured by the dogs. (*The Role of Slaves in Fifteenth-Century Turkish Romania*, by M. M. Alexandrescu-Dersca Bulgaru. Quoted in *Legacy of Jihad*, p. 568)

We have already learned that Muslims took slaves from the cities they conquered, but for about 1000 years the Muslims in North Africa also engaged in a systematic campaign of capturing Christian ships, plundering the cargo, and enslaving the crew and passengers; they also raided many European coastal towns.

Muslim Corsairs sailed as far north as Ireland and England to capture slaves. Some people were literally dragged out of churches and taken into slavery:

> Corsairs appeared off County Cork, Ireland, in 1631 and bore away 237 men, women, and children. Between 1613 and 1622, Algerian corsairs captured 447 Dutch ships. Four hundred English ships were taken in just four years, many right off the English coast. During six months in 1636, more than 1,000 Englishmen experienced the anguish of North African slavery. France wasn't spared, either. Between 1628 and 1634, eighty French ships and 1,331 men and women fell into the raiders' hands.
>
> . . . Long stretches of coastline were abandoned, and commerce, community life, and fishing declined as the people moved away, or were slain or spirited away into captivity. Spain and Italy reported losses of 300,000 to 500,000 inhabitants each late in the seventeenth century . . . (Wheelan, *Jefferson's War*, p. 17-18)

Some of the lucky ones were ransomed, but most people spent the rest of their lives as slaves. If the captured passengers or crew converted to Islam they would get jobs without hard labor. Those who were owned by the Sultan of Morocco and did not convert were literally worked to death, and usually did not live more than a year or two. European attempts to stop the barbarity with military action met with little success, so they preferred to pay the offending cities with gold and arms, which just better equipped them for more attacks.

The Muslims did everything in their power to force Christian slaves to convert, and took special pleasure in doing so from the moment the Christians stepped ashore. They were marched through the streets while the general population spat upon them, threw stones at them, and called them "dogs" and every other foul name that existed:

Throughout Barbary, there were <u>slave owners who pressurized [sic] their slaves into renouncing Christianity</u> and adopting the religion of their new land. They paid particular attention to their younger captives and gained great kudos from owning slave converts, particularly if they were masons, blacksmiths or professional soldiers. (Giles Milton, *White Gold*, 2004, p. 84)

It seems most of the architects, engineers, and tradesmen of all crafts were either slaves or apostates, called renegades, who converted to escape the brutally hard labor, frequent beatings, and bad food. The Muslims were intentionally cruel to the Christian slaves, making them live in dark underground rooms called slave pits or matamores, where they slept on mats that were crawling with lice and roaches: *"the matamores were usually 'filthy, stinking and full of vermin,' and death was all too often a blessed release"* (Ibid, p. 69).

The walls of a palace in Fes, Morocco, built by European slaves.

They were very poorly fed, and were worked from daylight to dark until they died. It is safe to say that 99.9% of the slaves had their feet bound together with a bastinado and raised from the ground; then they were beaten on the bottoms of their feet. They usually received 40 to 50 blows, but could receive as many as 500 (Ibid, page 83). Some received the bastinado beatings daily until they could no longer endure it and converted to Islam. The Muslims did this even to children.

One Thomas Pellow, age 11 or 12 at the time of capture, was thusly tortured every day and denied food and yet he would not renounce Christianity until *"burning my flesh off my bones by fire, which the tyrant did, by frequent repetitions, after a most cruel manner"* (Ibid, p. 84). He spent 23 years in captivity, but eventually escaped to tell his story.

The caption on this photo reads, *The morning's "entertainment" at the Kasbah, Tangier: Inflicting the bastinado,* (London News, Feb. 10, 1894).

The Moroccan sultans were very cruel to everyone, especially to the Christian slaves, and actually took pleasure in torturing and murdering them, often doing the bloody work themselves; *"violent beatings were common place"* (Ibid, p. 23). Milton quotes from a book written in 1627 or 1628, *The Tragicall Life and Death of Muley Abdala Melek*, by John Harrison:

> "He would cause men to be drubbed, or beaten almost to death in his presence," wrote Harrison, "[and] would cause some to be beaten on the soles of their feet, and after make them run up and downe among the stones and thornes." Some of the sultan's slaves had been dragged behind horses until they were torn to shreds. A few had even been dismembered while still alive . . . (Milton, *White Gold*, p. 23)

The sultan's son, Moulay Ismail, became as evil a sultan as his father. Moulay was skilled at mounting his horse and drawing his sword in one motion, and then cutting the head off the slave who was holding the stirrup (Ibid, p. 80).

The Muslims even captured American shipping, forcing a young United States to also pay off the robbers; but the U.S. usually did not have the funds, which prevented American ships from sailing in the Mediterranean. When Jefferson and Adams were ambassadors to European countries, they met together with the ambassador from Tripoli; they wanted to know why the Muslims were enslaving Americans because we had done nothing to provoke them. The Muslim ambassador answered:

> Abdrahaman said they didn't understand the fine points of Islamic jihad, as it was interpreted in Barbary. He proceeded to illuminate the ministers. "The Ambassador," Jefferson later wrote to Jay, "answered us that it was founded on the Laws of their Prophet, that it was written in their Koran, that all nations who should not have acknowledged their authority were sinners, that it was their right and duty to make war upon them wherever they could be found, and to make slaves of all they could take as Prisoners, and that every Musselman who should be slain in battle was sure to go to Paradise." (Wheelan, *Jefferson's War*, p. 40-41)

There you have it in black in white; the Muslims are not attacking Europe and America today because we insulted their prophet or invaded Iraq; it is the same reason they have been attacking since the founding of Islam, jihad, which includes great rewards for those waging jihad, such as plunder and sex slaves.

(4) Muslim Pirates

The Muslim pirates were not just some rogue men who went out on their own; no, they were sent out by Muslim nations. In 1793 the American Ship, Polly, was captured and its crew taken to Algiers and into slavery:

> Upon landing, the Americans were taken to the palace of the ruler, the dey of Algiers, through a surging crowd which stunned them "with the shouts, clapping of hands and other exclamations of joy from the inhabitants; thanking God for their great success and victories over so many Christian dogs, and unbelievers. . . ." The dey greeted them with a speech declaring he would never make peace with their country, finishing, "now I have got you, you Christian dogs, you shall eat stones." The next morning, a heavy chain link was hammered around each man's ankle . . . (Leiner, Frederick C. *The End of Barbary Terror: America's 1815 War Against the Pirates of North Africa*. Oxford U. Press, p. 3) (The inside quote is from, Foss, John, A Journal of the Captivity and Sufferings of John Foss; Several Years a prisoner at Algiers. Newburyport, Mass. 1798)

By 1801 Thomas Jefferson had enough of Islamic thuggery; within three weeks of becoming president he ordered American warships to the Mediterranean. (This war is actually what caused the creation of the U.S. Marine Corps.) The first battle was fought by the U.S. ship *Enterprise,* with a crew lacking experience, and disguised as a merchantman. It was attacked by a corsair with seasoned Muslims fighters, but the *Enterprise* destroyed the Muslim ship with cannon fire:

> . . . Porter grabbed hold of the lines, climbed aboard, and saw a dreadful sight: The deck was littered with dead and dying men, and the planks were slippery with blood. . . . Watching the surrender, Sterett ordered his men to board the Tripolino, which was now listing and taking on water. Stepping aboard, he, too, was repulsed by the carnage. Porter quickly gave him the tally:

twenty dead, including the surgeon and second officer, and thirty wounded, including the captain and first lieutenant. Sterett asked for the butcher's bill aboard his own ship and was stunned by the answer: none. In a battle that had lasted three hours, the Enterprise had taken the larger vessel without a single casualty. Nor, he found, had they suffered any significant damage. Sterett realized that he had just won a victory that would resonate throughout the Mediterranean, and the world. (*Tripoli*, by David Smethurst. p.87)

(This is what can happen when you have God fighting with you, but America no longer has God fighting on its side!)

In the next battle, the *Philadelphia* ran aground on a coral reef off the coast of Tripoli, so the captain surrendered, putting himself and the crew into slavery until a ransom was paid. The captured *Philadelphia* was raised by the tide and anchored in the harbor between other Tripolian ships and under the guns of the castle. In spite of the danger, not wanting the ship to be used against themselves, the U.S. sailed another ship into the harbor at night and used small rowboats to board the *Philadelphia*. In fierce hand-to-combat, the Americans killed twenty of the Muslims with only one American wounded, and set the *Philadelphia* on fire, and made their escape amid cannon and gunfire (Ibid, p. 174).

This was America's first war against Islamic terror (1801-1805), but it was poorly executed, and actually lost by the diplomats, so we had to go back again in 1815. This time we arrived with a fleet of ships and demanded a peace treaty or Algiers would be destroyed. This ended the problem for the U.S.

England also made a treaty with them, but when the English thought the treaty had been broken, they sent a relative of Thomas Pellow, Sir Edward Pellow, in 1816 to bombard Algiers, which was reduced to rubble by the fleet's cannon-fire:

Pellow himself was immensely proud of his role in destroying Algiers, and even more gratified when he was brought the news that Tunis, Tripoli and Morocco had also renounced [white] slavery. The great slave auctions were to be closed in perpetuity, and all of the remaining captives were freed without further ado. (Milton, *White Gold*, p. 276)

But this only ended the taking of slaves from Europe and the U.S.; slavery still existed throughout the Muslim world. Even though the English knew the pain and horror of slavery, the experience did not move them to end black slavery until 1833.

During World War I, the Turks of the Ottoman Empire used Christian and Jewish slaves to make their bombs and explosive shells. An American eyewitness reports how the Ottomans tortured their slaves in Jerusalem using the bastinado:

> The Ordnance Workshops occupied the commandeered English schools near the American Colony. In the late afternoon the reckoning took place for all the imaginary or real insubordination of the Christian and Jewish laborers [i.e. slaves]. They were lined up to watch their unfortunate companions being punished. The bastinado was generally used, which is a cruel chastisement. The victim was thrown on the ground and his feet made firm by twisting a rope around a stick with the feet in between. The stick was held by two men and the beating was on the soles of the feet. We could hear the screams of these wretched men from our house. (Vester, *Our Jerusalem*, p. 248)

Muslim countries were the last to officially end all slavery in the 20th century, and then only because of pressure from Western Europe and North America. The last was Saudi Arabia in 1962! But it has continued unofficially, underground.

(5) Other Kingdoms

The Crusaders (1096-1291) took back a very small part of the Middle East from the Muslims. Although they killed more than they should have killed, they did not invade in order to loot and plunder and sell people as slaves, or to oppress the population like all the empires did. After the conquest, the Crusaders usually ruled fairly and most people prospered, even Muslims:

> . . . the Spanish Muslim Ibn Jubayr (1145-1217), who traversed the Mediterranean on his way to Mecca in the early 1180s, found that Muslims had it better in the lands controlled by the Crusaders than they did in Islamic lands. Those lands were more orderly and better managed than those under Muslim rule, so that even Muslims preferred to live in the Crusader realms. (Spencer, *The Politically Incorrect Guide to Islam and the Crusades*, p. 131)

One reason the Muslims were better off under Crusader rule was the frequent warfare that took place among the Muslim factions as described above. Muslims eventually spread their rule from Morocco to the borders of China, making the empire the second largest in history. The Seljuk Turks invaded and conquered about half of the Middle East, but they ruled less than 200 years. The invading Crusaders helped the breakup of their empire.

The Turks had already converted to Islam before they invaded other Islamic regions, so they were not spreading Islam, but merely plundering and taking power. It was these Seljuks that the Crusaders fought for control of the Holy Land in the first and second Crusades (1098, and 1147). So the Arabic and Seljuk Islamic Empires were ruling at the same time, just different regions.

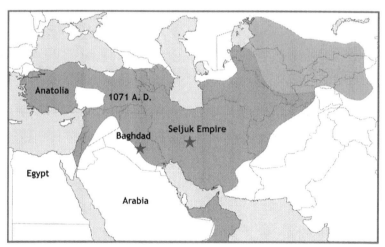

The Arabic Empire still retained a lot of territory, but because of all the power struggles that included murder and backstabbing (literally and figuratively), the Islamic rulers began buying Turkish slaves, called Mamluks, from northeast of Anatolia to populate the army in the 9th century. When the Egyptian sultan was killed by the French in 1250 during the 7th Crusade, the Mamluk slave warriors were powerful enough to defeat the Crusaders and take over the sultanate of Egypt. The caliphate was taken to

Egypt where it remained until the Ottomans invaded Egypt and transferred the caliphate to Anatolia in 1517.

The Mongol Empire was the largest continuous land empire in world history, stretching about 6,000 miles and encompassing China, most of Russia, and into Eastern Europe, as well as the nations west of India and just into the Middle East. It began in the 12th century under the leadership of Khabul Khan but became a true empire under the leadership of his son, Temujin, who was named Universal Ruler (Genghis Khan) of all the Mongol tribes in 1206 A.D.

The Mongol Empire invaded the Middle East but the Mamluks were strong enough to defeat them in a battle in 1260 which kept the Mongols from invading present day Lebanon, Israel, and Egypt. The Mamluks also drove out the Crusaders in 1291.

The Mongol invasion included many Turkish soldiers from south of Russia and their families who had joined the Mongols as they swept westward; they settled throughout Persia and Syria. Some of the Turks were already Muslims, and the Mongols within the Islamic regions eventually converted to Islam. After considering Christianity and Buddhism, and probably other religions, they chose Islam (no doubt because Islam is the most accepting of warfare, murder, and plunder).

Though the Mongols caused much devastation and slaughter during their invasions, within a couple of hundred years you would not have known they invaded, except for the lower population due to the large number of people they killed, because they did not impose a religion or language. The Mongol Empire suffered the same problems that the Arabic and Seljuk Turks suffered from: its large size and wars of succession caused the empire to fracture and it eventually just fell apart and was no more by 1368. So it lasted less than 200 years.

Chapter 4
The Ottoman Empire

(1) The Ottoman Turks

It was in about 1300 that a Turk named Osman began growing in power in northwestern Anatolia, which is present-day Turkey, just outside the Mongol controlled area. It took him and his
sons over 100 years to conquer Asia Minor, taking it from the
Eastern Romans. Then they spread from there, gradually creat-
ing the Ottoman Empire.

The Ottomans continued expanding with the usual burning,
raping, and enslaving until there was nothing left of the Eastern
Roman Empire. Satan's armies finally defeated the city of Constantinople in 1453, which then became Istanbul, ending 1100
years of Christian life and culture. Once the walls of the city were
breached, and the Muslims entered the city, what did they begin
doing to the helpless citizens? Murdering, raping, and looting, of
course:

> Sultan Mehmet had promised to his soldiers the three days of
> pillage to which they were entitled. They poured into the city . . .
> They slew everyone that they met in the streets, men, women
> and children without discrimination. The blood ran in rivers
> down the steep streets from the heights of Petra towards the
> Golden Horn. But soon the lust for slaughter was assuaged. The
> soldiers realized that captives and precious objects would bring
> them greater profit. (Runciman, Steven. *The Fall of Constantino-
> ple 1453*. p. 145)

Most of the survivors were destined for slavery, but they
could prevent such a fate by renouncing Christianity and adopt-

ing Islam. A few lucky ones were released after their relatives paid a ransom.

> Many other youths were offered liberty and commissions in his army on condition that they renounce their religion. A few of them apostatized; but the greater part preferred to accept the penalties of loyalty to Christ [death or slavery]. (Ibid, p. 149)

In case some Muslims want to dispute these facts, here is evidence from their own history books:

> He sent his messenger, Isma'il Hamzah Asfindyar Aughli, with a message to Emperor Constantine: resuming the war was of no avail, for the city would be defeated by force. It would be captured, its men would be killed, and the women and children would be captives or sold in the markets. . . .
>
> Forty thousand Christian Byzantines were killed in the siege and the attack. A large number of Greeks were killed and their children were taken by the Muslims to be taught the Arabic language and the Qur'an. The women were added to the harem of the Sultan and his men. (*The Islamic Openings*, by Abdul Aziz Al-Shinnawy, pages 341, 346)

According to Jewish tradition, Messiah is supposed to come through the eastern gate, so the Ottomans walled it up and put a cemetery in front of it in 1541.

The magnificent church called Hagia Sophia (Church of Holy Wisdom), built by Justinian, the grandson of Constantine, was turned into a mosque. Today it is a museum and tourist attraction, but there are now calls for it to become a mosque again.

The *Encyclopedia Britannica* says:

> The Ottoman Empire, one of the most powerful states in the world during the 15th and 16th centuries . . . came to an end only in 1922, when it was replaced by the Turkish Republic [1923] and various successor states in southeastern Europe and the Middle East. At its height it included most of southeastern Europe to the gates of Vienna, including modern Hungary, Serbia, Bosnia, Romania, Greece, and Ukraine; Iraq, Syria, Israel, and Egypt; North Africa as far west as Algeria; and most of the Arabian Peninsula. (v.28, p. 945)

The history of the Ottoman Empire is one of almost constant warfare against Christians and Jews and even other Muslims. They made several attempts to invade Western Europe but were stopped at the gates of Vienna. The third and final attempt was in 1683. Bosnia-Herzegovina, Serbia, and Croatia were mostly Christian for centuries, but when the Turks invaded they killed Christians and imported Muslim people to settle the regions. The conflict in the 1990s in these regions was the result of this past conflict.

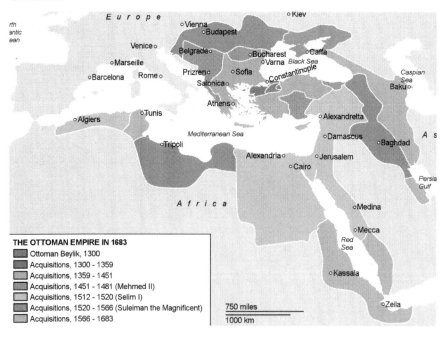

THE OTTOMAN EMPIRE IN 1683
- Ottoman Beylik, 1300
- Acquisitions, 1300 - 1359
- Acquisitions, 1359 - 1451
- Acquisitions, 1451 - 1481 (Mehmed II)
- Acquisitions, 1512 - 1520 (Selim I)
- Acquisitions, 1520 - 1566 (Suleiman the Magnificent)
- Acquisitions, 1566 - 1683

750 miles
1000 km

Even worse, when the Turks conquered a city, they took male children as captives, forced them to convert to Islam, and trained them to be a fighting force called Janissaries (Janizaries). The Janissaries were used to fight Christians. In some cases when a city was taken, part of its annual tribute included a certain number of male children. Sometimes the sultan's taxes were so high that the Christians could not pay them, and their only recourse was to give up one of their male children to be raised a Janissary. So we can now understand why there is so much hatred between the Christians and Muslims in the Balkans.

The Ottomans were especially barbaric and merciless. When the Arabians were fighting the Turks to gain their independence before World War I, if an Arab was wounded and could not ride his horse or camel to escape, his fellow tribesmen shot him to save him from the extreme tortures of the Turks.

The Ottoman Empire was conquered by the British Empire during World War I.

Greek drawing made between 1600 & 1800 shows the beast of the Ottoman Empire trying to eat the lamb of Christianity.

(2) Daniel 11: The King Who Exalts Himself

Daniel 11:36-45 is a passage that many Bible scholars believe refers to the final beast, the Antichrist. But the passage actually covers a long period of time from the beginning of Islamic aggression until the destruction of the Ottoman Empire. Therefore, the "king" spoken of actually refers to Satan, going by the name "Allah" and it also refers to a certain extent to Muhammad, who exalted the name "Allah."

> The king [Allah] will do as he pleases. He will exalt and magnify himself above every god and will say unheard-of things against the God of gods. He will be successful until the time of wrath is completed, for what has been determined must take place. (v. 36)

It was really Satan, behind the mask of Allah, who Muhammad exalted high above every other god, and blasphemed the Son of God. The last sentence of that verse tells us that Islam will continue as a powerful force in the world until the return of Christ. Islam will be destroyed by the wrath of God at the end of the Great Tribulation. Daniel 11 continues:

> 37 He will show no regard for the gods of his fathers or for the one desired by women, nor will he regard any god, but will exalt himself above them all.

When Muhammad took control of Mecca in 630 A.D. at the head of a 10,000-man army, he destroyed all the 360 idols inside the temple called the Kaaba. In so doing, <u>Muhammad did not regard the gods which his forefathers had worshiped, but destroyed them, and exalted Allah above them all.</u>

Notice the statement, *"or for the one desired by women."* Many translations, including the literal translations, say, *"nor for the desire of women."* Consider this: Islam is perhaps the most repressive belief system on the face of this planet toward women. Islam demeans them in many ways and considers them barely above infidel dogs; that is, Christians and Jews.

Whole books have been written detailing the mistreatment of women under Islam which allows men to beat their wives, divorce them at will, allows the male slave owners to rape their female slaves whenever they want, gives women half as much inheritance as men, calls women stupid, regards one man's testimony in court to be worth that of two women, allows for 24-hour marriages as a cover for fornication even with underage girls, and even gives the death penalty by stoning to a woman for having sex outside of marriage if she reports being raped (*The Sword of the Prophet*, by Trifkovic, p. 154). This still happens today! Sometimes she only gets 100 lashes, which she may not survive. All these atrocities are part of Islamic Law.

It has been common throughout Islamic history to marry a woman for just a few hours or days for sex, then divorce her. The memoir of a wife during the late 19th and early 20th centuries relates this fact:

> . . . her husband, who often traveled, acquired more wives on the road – a common practice among "traveling men": "During the annual haj season he had worked on the pilgrim ships bound for Arabia. He would marry a woman aboard ship and divorce her upon arrival. His marriages were so numerous he couldn't count them nor did he know the number of children he had. Meanwhile, I found him going after servant girls in the house." (*Harem: The World Behind the Veil*, by Alev Lytle Croutier, page 155)

Today in Iran there are thousands of women being abused; some are prostitutes, and / or heroin addicts, which puts them into a position where corrupt government officials can preyed upon them. *Front Page Magazine* reports these abuses:

> In Tehran, there are an estimated 84,000 women and girls in prostitution, many of them are on the streets, others are in the 250 brothels that reportedly operate in the city. The trade is also international: thousands of Iranian women and girls have been sold into sexual slavery abroad. . . .
>
> Many of these young women are actually being sold as sex slaves and taken to other Arab countries. The head of Iran's Interpol bureau believes that the sex slave trade is one of the most profitable activities in Iran today. This criminal trade is not conducted outside the knowledge and participation of the ruling fundamentalists. Government officials themselves are involved in buying, selling, and sexually abusing women and girls. . . .
>
> Popular destinations for victims of the slave trade are the Arab countries in the Persian Gulf. According to the head of the Tehran province judiciary, traffickers target girls between 13 and 17, although there are reports of some girls as young as 8 and 10, to send to Arab countries. One ring was discovered after an 18 year -old girl escaped from a basement where a group of girls were held before being sent to Qatar, Kuwait and the United Arab Emirates. (*Sex Slave Jihad*, By Donna M. Hughes, FrontPageMagazine.com, Jan. 27, 2004.)

Since Muslims no longer have access to a large supply of Christian girls to sell, they are now selling their own girls, a product of the low view of women in Islam. Muhammad said most people in hell are women. Clearly, Islam has no respect for women. They also engage in 91% of the world's honor killing of women and girls (*Middle East Quarterly*, Spring 2010, p. 3-11). Muslims even honor-kill women in Europe and the U.S., but get set to prison for it.

The *League of Nations* had a program after World War I that helped Christian women who had been kidnapped and forced into harems; in other words, they were sex slaves of the sultan, and later escaped:

> For years Miss Yappe had been repatriating Christian girls who had been kidnapped by Moslem Turks and Arabs and put into their harems . . . She told me the Armenian and Assyrian men married them without imputing any blame or disgrace to their lives, because they had been forcibly taken, and at great risk had returned. She told me that she had found homes for about ten thousand such women. (Vester, *Our Jerusalem*, p. 301)

If 10,000 Christian women had escaped in a decade or two, how many were kidnapped and forced into harems during the previous 1300 years? This stems from the Islamic rule that a man can only have four wives, but an unlimited number of sex slaves. Even today, thanks to the "Arab Spring," Christian girls are being kidnapped and forced into slavery in Egypt, Iraq, and Syria.

As recently as 1909 the Ottoman rulers had harems with up to 2,000 slave girls who sometimes sat around completely naked:

> Young girls of extraordinary beauty, plucked from the slave market, were sent to the sultan's court, often as gifts from his governors. . . . The girls were all non-Moslems, uprooted at a tender age. The sultans were partial to the fair, doe-eyed beauties from the Caucasus region. Circassians, Georgians, and Abkhasians . . . they were being kidnapped or sold by impoverished parents. (Croutier, *Harem: The World Behind the Veil*, p. 30)

You could buy 3-5 girls for the price of one horse. They usually ranged in ages from their lower teens, but were even as young as 8 years old. In the sultan's harem, lesbianism and sexual molestation of the young girls by the older women were known to occur (Ibid, p. 91).

Harem Servant, painted in 1874.

(The black squares were put there by the publisher to prevent a charge of child porn, and to not offend anyone.)

Throughout the Ottoman Empire the wives of Muslim men were cloistered. They rarely appeared in public, and then they were completely covered. That being the case, how do we have a history of seductive, half-dressed belly dancers? Some of them were the concubines (sex slaves) of sultans and sheiks. A girl danced to entertain her master and hoped to excite him to attain gifts or a night in bed with him which could result in her becoming a rich and powerful mother to her master's sons. But there were also slave women who danced to entertain customers. A European named Gustave Flaubert spent a year in Egypt (1849-1850):

> [He] kept a diary full of extremely erotic and sensuous detail: "Kuchuk shed her clothes as she danced. Finally she was naked except for a *fichu* which she held in her hands and behind which she pretended to hide, and at the end she threw down the *fichu*. . . . Finally, after repeating for us the wonderful step she had danced in the afternoon, she sank down breathless on her divan, her body continuing to move slightly in rhythm." This leads to an incredible night of passion with the *alme* (dancer) Kuchuk. (Croutier, *Harem*, p. 182)

These women were the forerunners of the strippers and pole dancers of today, yet Muslims like to point to Western nations as "decadent." The dancers were slaves in the same way that women are victims of sex trafficking today, and forced to work as strippers and prostitutes throughout the world. At least it is not an accepted part of society today as it was within the Muslim world for 1300 years.

Female servants (slaves) and concubines (sex slaves) were often topless, but the wives were totally covered. Ibn Battuta traveled throughout the Muslim world for more than twenty years in the fourteenth century, and encountered *"female slaves and servants who went stark naked into the court for all to see"* in Islamic Mali, Africa (*The Adventures of Ibn Battuta: A Muslim Traveler of the 14th Century*, by Ross E. Dudd. Univ. of Cal. Press, 1989, p. 303). He did not approve of this, but it shows that it was not limited to the Ottomans.

The newest form of abuse of women involves Palestinian men who rape one of their own, then give her the opportunity to cleanse her stained honor by becoming a suicide bomber.

If this information disturbs you, it should, because it shows just how evil Islam is, and is further evidence that Islam will be the religion of the final empire beast and final Antichrist. All of this abuse goes back to Muhammad who said his men could rape their captives, even the captive women who were married:

> Also forbidden are married women unless they are captives (of war). . . . (4:24) (*Sacred Writings, Islam: The Quran*, translated by Ahmed Ali, New York, 1992)

So it should come as no surprise that there is a rape epidemic in Europe, including gang rape. Not only are most rapes committed by Muslims, but such a large number of rapes are occurring that the police are not able to investigate them all. Europe is so paralyzed by far-left political correctness that they rarely report that an offender is a Muslim.

Sweden, Norway, UK, Belgium and other nations are already being ruled by Islamic Law because it is illegal to criticize Islam, and many aspects of Sharia Law are in place throughout the nations. Experts say that America is headed this direction and will be there in twenty years. (answering-islam.org/Silas/ femalecaptives.htm, www.gatestoneinsti tute.org/3854/uk-taxi-rapes, http://europenews.dk/en/node/63520, www.gatestoneinstitute.org/3442/ belgium-islamic-state, defendthemodernworld.wordpress.com/2013/07/23/ the-muslim-rape-war-against-europe)

(3) A God of Warfare

Daniel 11 continues:

> 38 Instead of them, he will honor a god of fortresses; a god unknown to his fathers he will honor with gold and silver, with precious stones and costly gifts.

A *"god of fortresses"* tells us that Allah is a god of war. It is with warfare that Islam was originally spread. CWD says:

> . . . is used in the expression "god of fortresses," indicating a god of war (Dan. 11:38). (*CWD Old Testament*)

As much as modern Muslims like to declare otherwise, any objective study of history will show that Islam was spread with the sword. One of the purposes of the warfare was to gain plunder. The Muslims plundered enormous quantities of gold and silver from the cities they attacked, especially from Persia and Egypt.

A book published in 1713 says:

> 6. In the Turkish prayers they use the following epithet of God;
> Rabol Maizza, the <u>Lord of Powers or Fortitudes</u>, which is the
> same with Eloah Mauzzi, Dan. 11:31, which is the title of God
> omnipotent, and the words of the prayer are these: *Be that far
> from you, O Lord, O Lord of Powers; which they* (Christians)
> *attribute to you,* (that you are a father, and has a wife and son).
> This is a public profession against the Father and Son, and the
> most evident character of Antichrist, and not of the pope.
> (Floyer, *The Sibylline Oracles*, p. 324-326)

This quote indicates that the Turks once had a prayer that included the phrase, *"the lord of powers,"* which is what it literally
says in Daniel. Interesting, to say the least. Daniel 11 continues:

> 39 He will attack the mightiest fortresses with the help of a for-
> eign god and will greatly honor those who acknowledge him. He
> will make them rulers over many people and will distribute the
> land at a price.

The Hebrew for "foreign" also means "pagan." Bishop New-
ton translated the last part of the verse this way; *"the earth he shall
divide for a reward."* The LXX says, *"shall distribute the land in
gifts."* The rulers who bowed to the Islamic sword without a fight
were handsomely rewarded. There were several occasions when
an individual would approach the Muslims and make a deal with
them; if they would reward him in some way, such as make him
the ruler or pay him with a huge sum of money or land, he
would tell them how they could easily defeat the city by exposing
a hidden entrance or by some other means. Daniel continues
with 11:40:

> "At the time of the end the king of the South will engage him in
> battle, and the king of the North will storm out against him with
> chariots and cavalry and a great fleet of ships. He will invade
> many countries and sweep through them like a flood."

In this passage, the king of the North was the Eastern Roman
Empire that ruled Anatolia, Syria, Palestine, and Egypt. The
king of the South was the ruler of Persia. These two had fought a
war with each other just before the rise of Islam, but here in verse

40 they both fight against someone else who is neither the king of the South nor the king of the North, called "him." Verse 40 states that the events take place "*at the time of the end*," but this can refer to the entire time since the coming of Christ, because even the first century was called the last days in Acts 2:17. The *him* refers to the Caliph of the Muslims, or perhaps Allah, who fought both the Persians and Eastern Romans and eventually defeated them both.

Notice the statement, "*He will invade many countries and sweep through them like a flood.*" The Muslim armies were amazingly successful in their wars of conquest. They suffered few defeats, especially for an army that was not trained or equipped like the armies of Persia or the Eastern Romans. The Muslim armies did not march in legions or in any kind of formation; they just rushed in like madmen. Perhaps only Alexander the Great can claim to have conquered more quickly. Daniel continues:

> 41 He will also invade the Beautiful Land. Many countries will fall, but Edom, Moab and the leaders of Ammon will be delivered from his hand. 42 He will extend his power over many countries; Egypt will not escape.

The "*Beautiful Land*" is the land of Israel that was invaded in 637. But some cities in the surrounding region did not put up a fight and therefore did not get slaughtered and plundered. When the Muslims showed up with their usual demands, some of these cities submitted to Muslim rule and paid the tax rather than fight:

> The palaces of the kings and nobles were luxurious and beautiful, and the first sight of them considerably impressed the simple Saracens. After a siege of some duration, Madain opened its gate, and its capitulation was followed by the submission of the entire country lying to the west of the Tigris. (*A Short History of the Saracens,* by Syed Amir Ali, New Delhi, India, 1926, p. 29).

We learned from this quote that the cities west of the Tigris were not destroyed, because they submitted. The Tigris is in Iraq, so the region west of the Tigris in Iraq and Jordan is the area of Edom, Moab, and Ammon. So Daniel 11 gives us an amazingly accurate description of the coming of Islam. Dan. continues:

> 43 He will gain control of the treasures of gold and silver and all the riches of Egypt, with the Libyans and Nubians in submission.

The Muslims conquered Egypt, Libya and Nubia, and today they are still Islamic. This is powerful evidence! The KJV and MEV say, *"the Libyans and the Ethiopians shall be at his steps."* It means that they will walk with him, which means they will join with him, or convert to Islam and then join him in jihad, which is exactly what happened.

The above verses in Daniel describe the beginning and progress of Islamic empire. The next verse jumps ahead and describes the end of Islamic empire, which is the end of the Ottoman Empire.

(4) The Armenian Genocide

> 44 But reports from the east and the north will alarm him, and he will set out in a great rage to destroy and annihilate many.

There is no indication from the text itself that there is a great gap here, but there most certainly is, because the next chapter describes the time of the Great Tribulation. And the context tells us that the time jump takes place here rather than at the chapter break.

In the early 20th century, European nations and Russia conspired to destroy the Ottoman Empire, which resulted in the Ottomans committing a massive slaughter of Christians within the Middle East and Armenia. So, this verse in Daniel describes events prior to and during WWI. Australia (the east) was instrumental in helping the British defeat the Turks.

This is how it happened: Because the Ottoman Empire was so corrupt and committed repeated atrocities against Christians, the European nations and Russia met together and decided to carve up the empire. Their plan was to completely eliminate the Ottoman Empire, and for there to be no nation at all under Turkish rule, not even Anatolia. The European nations and Russia had already fought several wars with the Turks during the 1800s and had already taken several nations away from them; France took Algeria, Italy took Libya, and Britain took Egypt. Russia said the Ottoman Empire was the *"sick man of Europe."* So during World War I the Turks were fearful for their very existence.

Many Armenian Christians (east of Turkey near Russia) were in distress because of persecution and oppression and were calling out to Russia for help. So, because of the plan to carve up the Ottoman Empire, the Turks went into a rage against the Christians who they believed were causing them the most trouble, and so began the genocide of the Armenians in 1915. It is estimated that 1 to 2 million Armenian Christians were not just slaughtered, but were subjected to horrendous tortures. It was part of an overall plan to kill every last Christian inside the Ottoman-controlled territories.

The Turks have committed numerous massacres of Armenian Christians; as a result of the massacre in 1896, the Christians on the Turkish-controlled island of Crete rose up against the Muslims, and Greece declared war on the Ottomans in April 1897. *Funk & Wagnalls New Encyclopedia* says Turkey committed,

> . . . atrocities that shocked the world, including massacres estimated to have caused the death of 200,000 Armenians in 1896 alone. . . . As World War I continued, Turkish atrocities against Armenians increased, and the reports of the atrocities finally led the government of the United States to send a formal note of protest to Turkey on Feb. 17, 1916. The massacres continued, however, and privations and famine added to the death list . . . (*Funk & Wagnalls New Ency.* V. 2, p. 287)

After the 1914-15 massacre, many Armenian refugees fled to America. The Turks deny this massacre today but it was documented by eyewitnesses and survivors. Books are still being written and documentary films made about it. Here is what the U.S. ambassador to the Ottoman Empire wrote about it:

> During the spring of 1914 they (the Ottoman government) evolved their plan to destroy the Armenian race. Now, as four of the Great Powers were at war with them and the two others were their allies, they thought the time opportune . . .

The facts contained in the reports received at the Embassy from absolutely trustworthy eyewitnesses <u>surpass the most beastly and diabolical cruelties ever before perpetrated or imagined in the history of the world</u>. The Turkish authorities had stopped all communication between the provinces and the capital in the naive belief that they could consummate this crime of ages before the outside world could hear of it. But the information filtered through the Consuls, missionaries, foreign travelers and even Turks. (*The Tragedy of Armenia*, by U.S. Ambassador to the Ottoman Empire, Henry Morgenthau)

The people were driven out into the desert in groups of several thousand each, and were marched along the roads until they died of heatstroke and dehydration. It was on these marches that most of the atrocities were committed.

Along the route to Adana and beyond, Turkish women were given the dagger (hanjar) to give the final stab to dying Armenians <u>in order to gain credit in the eyes of Allah as having killed a Christian</u>. (*Passage to Ararat*, by Michael J. Arlen, Ballantine Books, 1975. Quoted in, *The Sword of the Prophet*, by Serge Trifkovic, page 122)

The troops were told they could do anything they wanted with the women and girls; any that resisted were murdered on the spot. Some were forced to strip and crawl on the hot burning sand until their bodies were burnt. Roads leading into the desert were lined on both sides with dead bodies. The last quote above is evidence that Muslims have historically considered it an honor to kill Jews and Christians.

Some men and children were towed out to sea in boats and dumped overboard to drown, and women were even crucified (*Washington Post*, January 1st, 1918, page 2). A newspaper article dated Sept. 27, 1915 carried the headline, *The Depopulation of Armenia*. It reads in part:

The shocking news of the massacre, torture and deportation of Armenian Christians makes a special appeal to American sympathy and helpfulness. From numerous and reliable sources in Turkey it seems certain that this is not a matter of local disorders or petty oppression, but a systematic effort to extirpate the Armenian race. Thousands of families have been driven from their homes to starve upon the roads. Towns and villages have been divested of their inhabitants. Many are being put to torture <u>to force them to renounce their Christian faith</u>. Women are interned in the harems and <u>children are sold as slaves</u>.

These outrages cannot be excused on the ground of military necessity, for the regions devastated are in some cases beyond the reach of any possible Russian invasion and the Armenians have not manifested any disposition to revolt except where, as at Van, they have been driven to it in self-defense. . . . (*The Independent*, a weekly in New York)

The Armenian holocaust would be better remembered today, but the Jewish Holocaust in World War 2 overshadowed it. But let us not forget the Greeks, Nestorians, Syrians, and others who were also murdered by the Ottomans.

(5) In Memory Of The 50 Million Victims Of The Orthodox Christian Holocaust

While doing research for this book I came across an astonishing article detailing the slaughter of many Christian groups by the Ottomans that was researched and written by two Eastern Orthodox priests. It shows how the Ottomans murdered many more than just the Armenians. The next several pages are from the article, and reprinted by permission:

****

Researched by Rev. Archimandrite Nektarios Serfes of Boise, Idaho, U.S.A., October 1999. Written by Reverend Father Raphael Moore. Originally published by the Holy Transfiguration Greek Orthodox Church Sioux Falls, SD, Protopresbtyer Benjamin Henderson, Priest.

History Of Asia Minor: 1894-1923

During 1894-1923 the Ottoman Empire conducted a policy of Genocide of the Christian population living within its extensive territory. The Sultan, Abdul Hamid, first put forth an official governmental policy of genocide against the Armenians of the Ottoman Empire in 1894.

Systematic massacres took place in 1894-1896 when Abdul savagely killed 300,000 Armenians throughout the provinces. Massacres recurred, and in 1909 government troops killed, in the towns of Adana [a region] alone, over 20,000 Christian Armenians.

When WWI broke out the Ottoman Empire was ruled by the "Young Turk" dictatorship which allied itself with Germany. Turkish government decided to eliminate the whole of the Christian population of Greeks, Armenians, Syrians and Nestorians. The government slogan, *"Turkey for the Turks"*, served to encourage Turkish civilians [to attack Christians] on a policy of ethnic cleansing.

The next step of the Armenian Genocide began on 24 April 1915 with the mass arrest, and ultimate murder, of religious, political and intellectual leaders in Constantinople and elsewhere in the empire. Then, in every Armenian community, a carefully planned Genocide unfolded: Arrest of clergy and other prominent persons, disarmament of the population and Armenian soldiers serving in the Ottoman army, segregation and public execution of leaders and able-bodied men, and the deportation to the deserts of the remaining Armenian women, children and elderly. Renowned historian Arnold Toynbee wrote that "the crime was concerted very systematically for there is evidence of identical procedure from over fifty places."

The Genocide started from the border districts and seacoasts, and worked inland to the most remote hamlets. Over 1.5 million Armenian Christians, including over 4,000 bishops and priests, were killed in this step of the Genocide.

The Greek Christians, particularly in the Black Sea area known as Pontus, who had been suffering from Turkish persecutions and murders all the while, saw the Turks turn more fiercely on them as WWI came to a close. The Allied Powers, at a peace conference in Paris in 1919, rewarded Greece for her support by inviting Prime Minister Venizelos to occupy the city of Smyrna with its rich hinterlands, and they placed the province under Greek control. This action greatly angered the Turks. The Greek occupation was a peaceful one but drew immediate fire from Turkish forces in the outlying areas. When the Greek army farmed out to protect its people, a full-fledged war broke out between Greece and Turkey (the Greco-Turkish war). . . . Betrayed by the Allied Powers, the Greek military front, after 40 long months of war, collapsed and retreated as the Turks began again to occupy Asia Minor.

September 1922 signaled the end of the Greek and Armenian presence in the city of Smyrna. On 9 September 1922, the Turks entered Smyrna; and after systematically murdering the Armenians in their own homes, the forces of Ataturk turned on the Greeks whose numbers had swelled, with the addition of refugees who had fled their villages in Turkey's interior, to upwards of 400,000 men, women and children.

The conquering Turks went from house to house, looting, pillaging, raping and murdering the population. Finally, when the wind had turned so that it was blowing toward the sea so that the small Turkish quarter at the rear of the city was not in danger, Turkish forces, led by their officers, poured kerosene on the buildings and homes of the Greek and Armenian sectors and set them afire. Thus, any remaining live inhabitants of the city were flushed out to be caught between a wall of fire and the sea. The pier of Smyrna became a scene of final desperation as the approaching flames forced many thousands to jump to their death or to be consumed by fire.

The Allied warships and shore patrol of the French, British and American military were eyewitnesses to the events. George Horton, the American Consul in Smyrna, likened the finale at Smyrna to the Roman destruction of Carthage. He is quoted in Smyrna (1922, written by Marjorie Dobkin) as saying: " *Yet there was no fleet of Christian battleships at Carthage looking on a situation for which their governments were responsible.*" This horrible act unleashed the last phase of the genocide against the Christians of Turkish Asia Minor.

On 9 September 1997, a series of speakers and memorial services, honoring the memory of the 3.5 million Christians who were murdered by Turkish persecutions from 1894-1923, were held in the greater Baltimore Washington area. ... Not only was this the memorial of the Holocaust of Smyrna (now Izmir) and the martyrdom of Smyrna's Metropolitan Chrysostomos, but also of the 3.5 million Christians who perished during the first Holocaust of this century. But the events of 1922 are not an isolated incident. The atrocities committed by Turkish forces against a civilian population began before WWI and have never ended. This event seeks to expose the continuum of a Turkish campaign of persecution, deportation, and murder designed to rid Asia of its Christian populace.

GREEKS
    * 1914: 400,000 conscripts perished in forced labor . . .
    * 1922:100,000 massacred or burned alive in Smyrna
    * 1916-1922: 350,000 Pontions massacred or died during
    forced deportations
    * 1914-1922: 900,000 perish from maltreatment, starvation
    and massacres; total of all other areas of Asia Minor

    TOTAL: 1,750,000 Greek Christians martyred 1914-1922

ARMENIANS
    * 1894-1896: 300,000 massacred
    * 1915-1916: 1,500,000 perish in massacres and forced
    deportations (with subsidiaries to 1923)
    * 1922: 30,000 massacred or burned alive in Smyrna

TOTAL: 1,800,000 Armenian Christians martyred 1894-1923

SYRIANS AND NESTORIANS
    * 1915-1917: 100,000 Christians massacred . . .

Under the Ottoman Empire the Christians suffered a steady decline. Forced conversions to Islam, the abduction of children to serve in the fanatical Janissary corps, persecutions and oppression reduced the Christian population. Oppression intensified, leading to Genocide. Christian clergy were a constant target of Turkish persecution, particularly once the 1894 policy of Armenian genocide had been declared by sultan Abdul Hamid.

Victims of horrible torture, many Orthodox clergy were martyred for their faith. Among the first was Metropolitan Chrysostomos who was martyred, not just to kill a man but, to insult a sacred religion and an ancient and honorable people. Chrysostomos was enthroned as Metropolitan [archbishop] of Smyrna on 10 May 1910. Metropolitan Chrysostomos courageously opposed the anti- Christian rage of the Turks and sought to raise international pressure against the persecution of Turkish Christians. He wrote many letters to European leaders and to the western press in an effort to expose the genocide policies of the Turks. In 1922, in unprotected Smyrna, Chrysostomos said to those begging him to flee: "It is the tradition of the Greek Church and the duty of the priest to stay with his congregation."

On 9 September crowds were rushing into the cathedral for shelter when Chrysostomos, pale from fasting and lack of sleep, led his last prayer. The Divine Liturgy ended as Turkish police came to the church and led Chrysostomos away. The Turkish General Nouredin Pasha, known as the "butcher of Ionia", first spat on the Metropolitan and informed him that a tribunal in Angora (now Ankara) had already condemned him to death. A mob fell upon Chrysostomos and tore out his eyes. Bleeding profusely, he was dragged through the streets by his beard. He was beaten and kicked and parts of his body were cut off. All the while Chrysostomos, his face covered with blood, prayed: "Holy Father, forgive them, for they do not know what they are doing." Every now and then, when he had the strength, he would raise his hand and bless his persecutors; a Turk, realizing what the Metropolitan was doing, cut off his hand with a sword. Metropolitan Chrysostomos was then hacked to pieces by the angry mob.

Among the hundreds of Armenian clergy who were persecuted and murdered were Bishop Khosrov Behrigian and Very Reverend Father Mgrdich' Chghladian.

Bishop Behrigian (1869-1915) was born in Zara and became the primate [archbishop] for the Diocese of Caesarea/Kayseri in 1915. He was arrested by Turkish police upon his return from Etchmiadzin where he had just been consecrated bishop. Informed of his fate, the bishop asked for a bullet to the head. Deliberately ignoring his request, the police tied him to a "yataghan" where sheep were butchered and then proceeded to hack his body apart while he was still alive.

Father Chghladian was born in Tatvan. In May 1915, as part of the campaign of mass arrests, deportations and murders, the priest was tortured and displayed in a procession, led by sheiks and dervishes while accompanied by drums, through the streets of Dikranagerd. Once the procession returned to the mosque, in the presence of government officials, the sheiks poured oil over the priest and burned him alive.

Four of the martyred bishops who were murdered between 1921-1922 are today elevated to sainthood in the Greek Orthodox Church: They are, in addition to Metropolitan Chrysostomos, Bishops Efthimios, Gregorios and Ambrosios.

Bishop Efthimios of Amasia was captured by the Turkish police and tortured daily for 41 days. In the last days of his life he chanted his own funeral memorial until finally dying in his cell on 29 May 1921. Three days later a written order for his execution arrived from Mustafa Kemal (Ataturk).

Metropolitan Gregorios of Kydonion remained with his church until the end, helping 20,000 of his 35,000 parishioners escape to Mytilene and other free parts of Greece. On 3 October 1922, the remaining 15,000 Orthodox Christians were executed; the Metropolitan was saved in order to be buried alive.

Metropolitan Ambrosios of Moshonesion, along with 12 priests and 6,000 Christians, were sent by the Turks on a forced deportation march to Central Asia Minor. All of them perished on the road, some slain by Turkish irregulars and civilians, the remainder left to die of starvation. Bishop Ambrosios died on 15 September 1922 when Turkish police nailed horseshoes to his feet and then cut his body into pieces. (www.serfes.org/orthodox/memoryof.htm)

****

What you have just read shows the truth about the character of Islam and the character of Turkey, and it will happen again when the Ottoman Empire rises from the Abyss.

Daniel 11 continues:

> 45 He shall pitch the tabernacles of his palace between the seas in the beautiful holy mountain. Yet he shall come to his end, and no one shall help him. MEV

Constantinople had been the capital of the Christian Roman Empire for 1,000 years. When it was defeated in 1453, it became the capital of the Ottoman Empire. Eventually, a great palace was built in perhaps the best location, between two seas. See map below.

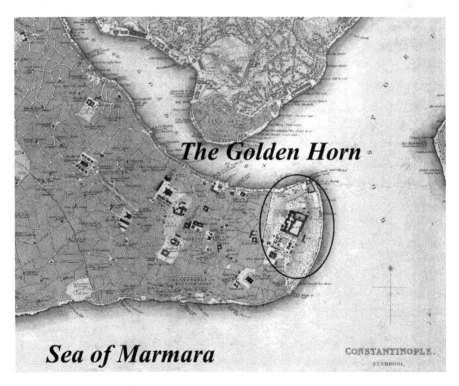

Notice the location of the palace. It is literally between two seas and is perhaps the most beautiful spot in all of Istanbul. The view is breathtaking. Today, the palace is a museum. The last part of the verse says, "Yet he shall come to his end, and no one shall help him." No one helped the Ottoman Empire during World War I and it was defeated (Germany was not able to help).

Though the Ottoman Empire was defeated, they fought hard to continue to exist and instituted reforms, so the Turkish people were allowed to have a homeland, which is the nation of Turkey today. It officially became the Republic of Turkey in 1922. The caliphate was abolished in 1924.

Even though the constitution of modern Turkey allows a certain amount of religious freedom, it continues trying to eliminate Christianity by confiscating thousands of church properties and looting them of antiques and icons which are sold through European auction houses. It also encourages the Muslim population to persecute Christians. In 1974, a supposedly moderate Turkish government invaded Cyprus. The operation was code named *Operation Attila*, apparently in honor of that great peacemaker Attila the Hun (irony in use). Turkey partitioned the island and displaced thousands of Greek Cypriots and burned churches or turned them into mosques.

We have seen that Daniel 11 refers to Islam's rise to power through the Arabic Islamic Empire, its rapid spread, and finally the end of Islamic empire in World War I. This, of course, does not show the end of Islam but merely the end of the Islamic beast that then existed. The Ottoman Empire was killed during World War I largely by the British Empire.

(6) The Conflict Continues

Here are some samples of recent news headlines that show the persecution of Christians by Muslims and the rise of radical Islam:

* Pakistani mob torches dozens of Christian homes
* Islam or death? Egypt's Christians targeted by new terror group
* Nigeria: Muslims gun down five Christians returning home from church

* Up to 100,000 Christians have fled Muslim Brotherhood Egypt
* Somalia: Muslims murder Christian on suspicion of his being an apostate from Islam
* Bangladesh: 46 dead as Muslims continue to riot over death sentence for Islamic supremacist leader
* Mass Arrest and Torture of Christians in Libya
* Burned Church Is Latest in String of Tanzanian Attacks
* France: Muslim smashes up church, leaves Qur'an and prayer rug inside, writes "Allahu akbar" on smashed statues
* Christians in Syria Targeted for Kidnapping
* India: Muslims murder 13, injure 84 with bombs in crowded area of Hyderabad
* Muslim mob stones Christians, sets church building on fire in Egypt
* Jihad murder in New Jersey? Coptic Christians beheaded, hands cut off
* Nigeria: Muslim jihad group murders three South Korean doctors, beheading one
* Syria: Jihadist rebels loot Christian church, homes
* Mali: Women whipped for having cellphone images of pop stars, venturing out unveiled
* Egyptian Court Gives Family 15 Years in Prison for Converting to Christianity
* All Churches in Historic Christian Town of Maaloula Either Destroyed or Desecrated (in Syria)
* Global Persecution of Christians Doubled In 2013, With Syria Accounting For Half Of Killings
* Bethlehem: One stabbed as Muslim mob storms and stones church
* Criticism of Islam forbidden by Toronto District School Board
* Syria: Islamic jihadist enters monastery, shoots elderly priest in the head
* Al-Qaeda Declares "We Must Eliminate the Cross"
* Open Season on Christians in Libya
* Muslim Girl, 14, Lashed to Death for Adultery (i.e. for being raped)

* Kenya: Muslim cleric accused of not supporting jihad teaching shot dead
* Jewish Teens Escape Axe Attack [by Muslims] Near Paris
* Pakistan: Islamic jihadists murder 27 as they take over the nation's busiest airport
* Palestinian Muslims in the Middle East Digging up Christian Bodies From Cemeteries and Burning Them

That last news headline is truly shocking. *Jewish News* (http://www.jewsnews.co.il/) in Israel reported that the Muslims are burning the corpses of dead Christians because the Muslims claim the bodies "defile" the land.

(7) The Myth of Peaceful Coexistence

Modern Muslims want you to believe that Jews and Christians have lived in peaceful coexistence with Muslims for centuries, but the facts of history speak otherwise. After the Muslims take over a country they engage in heavy taxation and daily discrimination and persecution, but only on a small scale until the Muslim population grows. The larger the Muslim population, the greater the persecution of the non-Muslims. Here is a historical timeline of sorts, showing the major incidents against the Jews in just one place, Morocco. It can be repeated for dozens of other nations in the Muslim world, and for Christians as well:

70 A.D.: Wave of Jewish immigration to Morocco following destruction of Second Temple in Jerusalem.

694: Queen Kahaina leads Berbers against invading Arab armies, but Islam wins. The result is that an entire group of Jews apostatized and became Muslims (*The adventures of Thomas Pellow, of Penryn, Mariner*, by Thomas Pellow, 1890, from the introduction by Dr. Robert Brown). This means they were at the very least threatened or they would not have converted.

695-1032: No officially documented killings. (In 695 the Muslim population was small, but grows.)

1033: 6,000 Jews killed in Fez by Muslim mobs.

1106: Ali ibn Yusuf ibn Tashifin founds Marrakesh, decrees

death penalty for local Jews even as his military leader and physician are Jews.

1107: Almoravide ruler Yusuf ibn Tashifin orders Jews to convert or be expelled from Morocco.

1148: Almohadin become rulers of Morocco, offer Christians and Jews the choice of conversion or expulsion. Many Jews convert, but continue to practice Judaism in secret.

1165: Almohad ruler declares all Jews must convert to Islam. Judah ha-Kohen ibn Shushan burned alive for refusing to convert. Maimonides flees Fez for Egypt.

1276: Riots targeting Jews of Fez stopped by Sultan.

1438: Jews of Fez forced into mellah (ghetto).

1465: Massive anti-Jewish rioting in Fez spreads across Morocco. Hundreds murdered. Only 11 Jews left alive in Fez.

1492: Jews fleeing Spanish Inquisition settle in Morocco.

1557: Marrakesh ghetto for Jews established.

1682: Meknes ghetto established.

1790: Pogrom in Tetouan: All Jews stripped naked, many women raped, most homes ransacked.

1808: Mulay Suleiman orders Jews of Tetuan, Rabat, Sale, and Mogador into ghettos.

1815: Jews of Mogador ordered to pay sudden jizya poll-tax. Those who pay are punched on the forehead, those who refuse are thrown in dungeon.

1834: "Suleika affair": Jewish woman from Tangier refuses to convert and marry a high-ranking official. She is executed.

1884-1888: 307 Jews murdered over four years by Muslims, but no Muslims put on trial.

1903: 40 Jews killed by Muslim riots in Taza. More killed in Settat.

1907: In Casablanca, 30 Jews killed, 200 women, girls and boys abducted, raped, then ransomed.

1910: Twelve-year-old grandson of Fez's Rabbi Abensur abducted and forcibly converted to Islam.

1912: Muslim rioters massacre 60 Jews in Fez, leave 10,000 homeless [must have burned entire ghettos].

1941: France's Vichy government implemented anti-Jewish laws in Morocco, a few internment camps for Jews briefly opened.

1942: Synagogues in Casablanca desecrated in anti-Jewish riots. Allied forces liberate Morocco.

1948: Jewish population approximately 285,000. French officials ban emigration of Moroccan Jews to Israel. Muslim riots in Oudjda and Djerada kill scores of Jews, wound 150.

1949-1956: Over 90,000 Jews emigrate from Morocco to Israel.

1952: Anti-Jewish mob violence. Jews flock to major cities, with 30,000 crowding Casablanca ghetto.

1954: Pillaging of Jewish property and destruction of Jewish schools across country, including a pogrom in Petitjean.

1956-1961: 18,000 Jews smuggled out of Morocco.

1957: Exit visas for Jews abolished.

1958: Morocco joins Arab League, forbids any Jewish emigration. All Zionist activity forbidden.

1960: Many Jewish schools nationalized.

1961: On the occasion of Egyptian President Nasser's visits to Casablanca, Jews beaten and arrested.

1961-1964: 80,000 Jews leave on chartered planes and ships in return for "compensation" to Moroccan government from Hebrew Immigrant Aid Society.

1965: Government permits the publication of the "Protocols of the Elders of Zion" [a publication used by Hitler and others to incite anti-Semitism].

1975: 22,000 Jews remain in Morocco.

2000: 6,000 Jews remain in Morocco; an estimated 600,000 Moroccan Jews and their descendants live in Israel.

2003: Jewish community center in Casablanca bombed as part of an Al Qaeda attack. (www.theforgottenrefugees.com)

****

The above only listed the major persecutions of Jews, not the daily small attacks that individuals must endure. Nor does it relate the persecutions of the Christians. A comment by Marco Polo in his book, *The Travels of Marco Polo*, is very revealing about what life was like for Christians and Jews in the 14th century:

> The Mahometan inhabitants are <u>treacherous and unprincipled</u>. According to their doctrine, <u>whatever is stolen or plundered from others of a different faith, is properly taken, and the theft is no crime;</u> whilst those who suffer death or injury by the hands of Christians, are considered as martyrs. If, therefore, they were not prohibited and restrained by the powers who now govern them, they would commit many outrages. <u>These principles are common to all the Saracens.</u>
>
> When they are at the point of death, their priest attends upon them, and asks whether they believe that Mahomet was the true apostle of God. If their answer be that they do believe, their salvation is assured to them; and in consequence of this facility of absolution, which gives free scope to the perpetration of everything flagitious, they have succeeded in <u>converting to their faith a great proportion of the Tartars, who consider it as relieving them from restraint in the commission of crimes</u>. (chapter 9)

The statements by Maro Polo also show the character and nature of those who follow Islam. An article published in 1888 titled, *"Palestine Fifty Years Ago and Palestine Today,"* shows us what life was like for Christians and Jews in the 1830s:

> The Jews, as well as the native Christians, throughout Syria and Palestine, were daily and hourly subjected to oppression, extortions, exaction, robbery and insults from their Moslem neighbours. It was no unusual occurrence for the Moslem to enter their houses, ransack closets and boxes, and appropriate any article of wearing apparel, furniture, or food that took the marauder's fancy.
>
> The local Government authorities would occasionally, when in need of funds, levy blackmail to the amount of hundreds of pounds on the Jews and native Christians, threatening them with massacre and plunder in default of payment. Consequently, Jews and native Christians dared to make any display of wealth only at the risk of losing life or property, and often both. . . . (*Aroha News* (New Zealand), October 24, 1888. Also, June 9, 2014 *Life in Palestine 1830-1880 as Described by a Very Unusual Woman, Lydia Mamreoff von Finkelstein Mountford*, www.israel dailypicture. com/2014/06/life-in-palestine-18 30-1880-as.html?)

A book titled, *Beyond the Bascilica: Christians and Muslims in Nazareth,* reveals how Christians were treated in Nazareth:

> That same year, a Christian girl, in rebuffing advances from a Muslim boy, was accused of blasphemy against the prophet Mohammad. Her sentence was to either convert to Islam or die. She chose to die, and execution was carried out by tying her to a horse and dragging her through the streets. (Emmett, page 24)

Although there were times when Christians and Jews did co-exist peacefully, yet unequally with Muslims, the majority of the time there was no peace. Even the day-to-day lives of Christians and Jews were filled with repressive discrimination.

Now for a more recent example of persecution and murder of Christians at the hands of Muslims in 1991 from *The New Foxe's Book of Martyrs*:

> Mary Khoury was 17 when her village in Lebanon was raided by Muslims who were bent on converting everyone to Islam by force. She and her parents were given one choice: "If you do not become a Muslim you will be shot." . . . she replied, "I was baptized as a Christian and His word came to me: 'Don't deny your faith.' I will obey Him. Go ahead and shoot." A Muslim who had just killed her father and mother shot her and left her for dead. Two days later the Red Cross came into her village. They found Mary and her family where they had been shot-- she was the only one alive. But she was now paralyzed, the bullet had severed her spinal cord. . . . (Chadwick, p. 349-350)

These incidents are not isolated, but occur in all countries where Muslims are in the majority. The incidents are in fact growing more numerous as the Muslims are becoming more Fundamentalist because of the influence of the Muslim Brotherhood. Several books and news articles have been written recently, detailing the growing persecution and massacre of Christians, especially in Egypt, Iraq, and Syria.

The *Free Syrian Army* (FSA), was backed by Obama; they murdered many Christians and burned their homes. WorthyNews.com reported in July, 2013 that the FSA went into the Christian village of Oum Sharshouh and burned down houses and terrorized the population, forcing 250 Christian families to flee. Two days later another attack was reported. The Christian village of al-Duwayr/Douar, south of the city of Hims and close to Lebanon's northern border, was invaded by the FSA:

> Around 350 armed militants forcefully entered the homes of Christian families who were all rounded-up in the main square of the village and then summarily executed. (*Free Syrian Army Massacre Christian Village,* July 5, 2013. worthynews.com)

Robert Spencer reported in *Front Page Magazine*:

> In September 2013, a day after Secretary of State John Kerry praised the Free Syrian Army as "a real moderate opposition," the FSA took to the Internet to post videos of its attack on the ancient Syrian Christian city of Maaloula, one of the few places where Aramaic, the language of Jesus, is still spoken.

> This is just the faction Obama is backing. The rebel factions funded by our "allies" Saudi Arabia, Qatar and Turkey behave even worse toward the Christians. (frontpagemag.com/2014/robert-spencer/u-s-vs-christians/)

For more reading on this subject, I recommend *Crucified Again: Exposing Islam's New War on Christians* by Raymond Ibrahim.

(8) A Final Word

Consider this: Islam has in the past, made war against Christian cities, and they are even now making war against Christian cities in Syria, and Islam's primary means of execution has always been decapitation. Muhammad said to strike the necks of those who oppose the spread of Islam, which is why Saudi Arabia still executes people by beheading:

> And I saw the souls of those who had been beheaded because of their testimony for Jesus and because of the word of God. They had not worshiped the beast or his image and had not received his mark on their foreheads or their hands. (Rev. 20:4)

Beheading does not apply to all previous empires; Rome favored crucifixion and the Mongols favored suffocation. The final empire will continue with beheading. Christians in Egypt and Syria are even now being beheaded and crucified. You would think that a modern empire would prefer to use a firing squad, but Islam is literally out of a dark cave where Muhammad was given his first revelations, and will never see the light of reason.

The TV news stations such as ABC, CBS, and NBC only occasionally report on the killing of Christians and burning of churches around the world. If you want to know what is happening on this subject, visit online news websites such as:

www.christianpost.com	The Christian Post
www.pjmedia.com	P. J. Media
www.indcatholicnews.com	Independent Catholic News
www.frontpagemag.com	Front Page Magazine
www.jihadwatch.org	Jihad Watch, by Robert Spencer
www.clarionproject.org	Clarion Project
www.gatestoneinstitute.org	The Gatestone Institute: International Policy Council
www.thereligionofpeace.com	The Religion of Peace

The last website includes lists of Islamic terrorist attacks that happen around the world. And the list is long <u>every month</u>.

This picture was taken in Trafalgar Square, London, Aug. 21, 2011. Britain has allowed so many Muslims into the country, and allowed them to live under Sharia Law, that Britain is close to being conquered by Islam. It is already illegal to criticize Islam, or even offend Muslims, in England.

Chapter 5
The Revived Ottoman Empire

(1) The Scarlet Beast

The Scarlet Beast described in Revelation 17 has the same seven heads and ten horns that are on the beast of Revelation 13; this is because it is actually the eighth head of that same beast. As we have seen, there is no head of the beast today, because the beast is currently dead. Islam is not dead, but there is no Islamic empire. But in Rev. 17 we learn that the beast will rise again, and will have a red color. Even though the color of Islam is green, the color of martyrdom is red, as was the color of the Ottoman Empire, and Turkey today.

> 3 Then the angel carried me away in the Spirit into a wilderness. There I saw a woman sitting on a scarlet beast that was covered with blasphemous names and had seven heads and ten horns. . . . 8 The beast, which you saw, once was, now is not, and will come up out of the Abyss and go to its destruction. The inhabitants of the earth whose names have not been written in the book of life from the creation of the world will be astonished when they see the beast, because it once was, now is not, and yet will come. (Rev. 17:3, 8)

We have already learned that the beast represents empires; in the above passage, the beast is dead. Rev. 17 explains the seven heads to us, and refers to the entire beast, not merely a leader.

It is saying that the beast, which is seven or more empires, will cease to exist; it will die, but it will come to life again, which is what is portrayed to us symbolically when we see the beast rise from the Abyss. Then it gives us more details; it tells us that when the beast rises again it will be the eighth head:

> The beast who once was, and now is not, is an eighth king. He belongs to the seven and is going to his destruction. (R.17:11)

The *Good News Bible* is more clear:

> And the beast that was once alive, but lives no longer, is itself an eighth king who is one of the seven and is going off to be destroyed. (GNB)

This tells us that the final ruling empire will be one of the former empires, revived. One of the seven heads will come back to life, making it the eighth king in succession but one of the previous seven. Therefore, you can identify the final head of the beast by studying history. Which one of the empires will it be? It will be the head that was killed in warfare.

> One of the heads of the beast seemed to have had a fatal wound, but the fatal wound had been healed. The whole world was astonished and followed the beast. (Rev. 13:3)

This passage does NOT refer to the Antichrist being killed by a head wound and coming back to life again; that is total nonsense. Remember what has been proven thus far, that the beast is an empire, not a person. The heads represent all the empires that have ruled, not individual rulers of those empires.

The fatal wound is not healed immediately after it was wounded, though you could come to that conclusion based on the wording of 13:3, but the wording in Rev. 17 indicates that there will be a gap between when it is killed and when it comes back to life; "*The beast, which you saw, once was, now is not, and will come up out of the Abyss.*" If you say, the beast once lived, but now does not live, but will live again, then there must be a space of time between when the beast is killed and when it comes to life again. The whole world will be astonished when they see the formation of the next Islamic empire.

Notice that this empire was killed by a wound; this indicates that it did not dissolve itself like the British Empire, or slowly get eaten away like the Eastern Roman Empire, but it was killed in a major war.

The Babylonian Empire was given a sudden death-blow in one day; then the Media-Persian Empire was defeated in a matter of days by Alexander the Great, and his empire was not defeated but split into four parts that had separate historical timelines. Those Greek empires were gradually conquered over the centuries by Rome, the Parthians, and even the Jews were able to throw off Seleucid Greek power in the Maccabean revolts, until nothing was left of the Seleucid Greek empire but a small area in Syria.

The Ottoman Empire was wounded in the mid-1800s and was given the deathblow during World War I. So the only possible empires that could rise out of the Abyss are the Babylonian, Media-Persian, or Ottoman. The regions of all three empires are Islamic today. Therefore, it is certain that the eighth and final empire will be Islamic. The largest, most powerful, and cruelest of these empires was the Ottoman. It was also the most recent, so it is the empire that will rise again. Therefore, the scarlet beast will be the revived Ottoman Empire, although it *may* have a different name.

When the Ottoman Empire became the nation of Turkey, their flag had only a small change; the removal of crossed swords.

(2) Ten Horns

The eighth head of the beast will be ten separate nations that join together to form an empire. The past empires became empires by a single city or nation invading and conquering other cities and nations and gradually growing into empires, which the Ottomans also did. But the Ottoman Empire was so large that it could not rule without local rulers, so it became mostly self-ruling nations who were paying tribute to the Ottoman sultans.

Did you notice in previous chapters, that Jefferson and Adams met with the ambassador from Tripoli? Why would a mere region of an empire send out ambassadors to foreign countries? Does Kansas host embassies from other nations and have embassies in other nations? No. If Tripoli was a mere state of the Ottoman Empire then it would not have hosted ambassadors and sent them out, both of which it did.

Likewise, the Revived Ottoman Empire will also be an association of nations. Rev. 17 provides more information about the ten horns:

> 12 "The ten horns you saw are ten kings who have not yet received a kingdom, but who for one hour will receive authority as kings along with the beast. 13 They <u>have one purpose</u> and will <u>give their power and authority to the beast</u>. 14 They will <u>make war against the Lamb</u>, . . . 17 For God has put it into their hearts to accomplish his purpose by agreeing to give the beast their power to rule, until God's words are fulfilled. (Rev. 17:12-14, 17)

Notice that the ten horns all "agree" to give the beast their power to rule. This means they join together to form an empire, thus becoming the eighth head of the beast. The text does not say that their purpose is to give their power and authority to the beast, but that they have the same purpose; it says "they *have one purpose* AND *will give their power and authority . . .*" (NIV). The NKJV says, "*These are of one mind.*" Their one purpose is to make Islam the dominant world political and religious power and to "*make war*" against Christians and Jews, and to destroy Israel, America, and Europe.

Even though Islam has historically slaughtered many Christians and Jews, it did not kill them all, but lived with many of them. However, Islamic teaching says that when the Muslim Jesus returns he will require all Christians to convert to Islam or be killed. This means that the final jihad will be much worse than all the jihad wars in history. People will no longer be asked to accept Islam, or pay a tax, or fight, they will be required to convert or die fighting. Islamic teaching says that by the end of the Day of Judgment, all Jews will have been killed by Muslims.

Rev. 17 says, "*They will make war against the Lamb*" (17:14). Some Bible prophecy "experts" teach that the armies of Antichrist will aim their guns into the sky in an attempt to shoot Jesus out of the sky when he returns! When Jesus struck down Saul on the road to Damascus, Jesus said *"why are you persecuting me?"* Since Saul was persecuting Christians, he was persecuting Christ, so when it says the beast makes war against the Lamb, it really means a war against Christians. No other religion has waged a literal war against Christians and Christianity, except Islam, and it will do so again. Communism and paganism have persecuted Christians, but it was not a literal war with soldiers fighting Christians.

These ten horns are not the same ten horns that are described in Daniel 7. The ten horns mentioned in Daniel 7 are not in agreement, or three would not be uprooted by the little horn. Therefore, the horns in Daniel are different from those in Rev. (this was fully explained in Book 1). Rev. repeatedly mentions ten horns and makes no mention of three that are not in agreement or are uprooted; all ten are in full agreement. No information is missing from Revelation.

In Psalm 83 we are told of a group of nations that make an agreement together to destroy Israel. Many people teach that this war will be a separate war, or perhaps starts the Great Tribulation, but it is not separate from the beast of Revelation's war, because it is actually a prophecy of the final beast. The nations named in Psalm 83 are all Islamic nations of the Middle East that surround Israel today:

> 2 See how your enemies are astir, how your foes rear their heads.
>
> 3 With cunning they conspire against your people; they plot against those you cherish.
>
> 4 "Come," they say, "<u>let us destroy them as a nation</u>, that the name of Israel be remembered no more."
>
> 5 With <u>one mind</u> they plot together; <u>they form an alliance</u> against you—
>
> 6 the tents of Edom and the Ishmaelites, of Moab and the Hagrites, 7 Gebal, Ammon and Amalek, Philistia, with the people of Tyre.
>
> 8 Even Assyria has joined them to lend strength to the descendants of Lot. (Psalm 83)

The passage says the same as Revelation 17, that they are all of "*one mind*," which means they are in agreement, and that they combine together to form an empire; "*they form an alliance.*"

A large part of the Book of Enoch is concerned with the last days, especially the Great Tribulation, as it says at the start of the book, "*The word of the blessing of Enoch, how he blessed the elect and the righteous, who were to exist in the time of trouble . . .*" It contains a passage that is very similar to the above passage in Psalm, and the context is clearly the last days:

> 9 Then shall princes <u>combine together</u>, and <u>conspire</u>. The chiefs of the east, among the Parthians and Medes, shall remove kings, in whom a spirit of perturbation [anxiety] shall enter. They shall hurl them from their thrones, springing as lions from their dens, and like famished wolves into the midst of the flock. . . . 12 In those days shall the mouth of hell be opened, into which they shall be immerged; hell shall destroy and swallow up sinners from the face of the elect. (*The Book of Enoch Updated*, by Richard Laurence, Chap. 54)

What Enoch said is taking place today with the Arab Spring, "*shall remove kings, in whom a spirit of perturbation* [anxiety] *shall enter. They shall hurl them from their thrones.*" The prophet Zechariah also prophesied on this subject, that many nations surrounding Israel will attack Israel, but will end up bringing destruction upon themselves:

> "I am going to make Jerusalem a cup that sends <u>all the surrounding peoples</u> reeling. Judah will be besieged as well as Jerusalem. 3 On that day, when all the nations of the earth are gathered against her . . ." (Zech. 12:2-3)

The above passages show that the enemies of Israel will be the nations surrounding Israel. There is no evidence that WW3 will come from Europe, or be caused by any European ruler or revived Roman Empire. The Psalm 83 war will NOT take place at the start of the Great Trib., but is the main war.

Is it a coincidence that the Prophet's Mosque in Madina, Saudi Arabia has ten spires that look very much like horns? (See photo below.) All the horns are part of this mosque, not other buildings; I have examined numerous photos.

Nations that could be one of the ten horns are: Turkey, Iraq, Iran, Syria, Jordan, Saudi Arabia, Kuwait, Lebanon, Oman, Qatar, United Arab Emirates, Egypt, Libya, Algeria, Sudan, Morocco, Turkmenistan, Uzbekistan, Tajikistan, Afghanistan, Pakistan, and others. Most of the ten horns will be made of nations that were once part of the old Ottoman Empire, but they will invade others that were not part of the empire (see Book 1 on the little horn).

(3) The Beast Rises

Since WWI the Turkish government tried to be a European nation and promoted modernism within the country, but it is now turning back to Ottomanism, back toward Islam and empire. During the 20th century, the ruling elite of Turkey wanted the country to be a secular state that is more like Europe than the Muslim Middle East. Ottomanism was even illegal until recently, much in the way that Nazism became illegal in Germany after World War 2. But now people can once again display the emblems of the Ottoman Empire. In 2012 Turkey minted its first coin without the face of Ataturk, the founder of modern Turkey. This was also seen by some people as a sign that Turkey is moving back to its Ottoman roots.

Previous empires are long gone; nothing remains except lines on a map or ancient buildings and artifacts, but the Ottomans still exist in Turkey. In fact, its current ruler is an Ottoman. In 2002, Recep Tayyip ~~Erdoğan, a~~ descendant of the Ottoman rulers, was elected Prime Minister. Since Turkey has been denied entry into the EU, it is now trying to become a major player in the affairs of the Middle East, and desires to become a leader in the Muslim world. So it is no surprise that Turkey, which has been a friend of Israel in the past, has recently become an enemy. Turkey condemned the Israeli offensive into Gaza in Jan. 2009, and Erdoğan denounced Israeli President Shimon Peres in a public debate in 2009 at the World Economic Forum in Switzerland. Erdoğan stormed out of the conference and arrived home to a hero's welcome:

> People who have been paying attention know that relations between Israel and Turkey have been eroding, but not many realize that Turkey is now not only openly hostile to the Jewish State, but also to the Jewish people. (Lori Lowenthal Marcus, Jan. 15, 2013. www.jewishpress.com)

Erdoğan is not only an Ottoman, his government is seen by many as Islamist because it contains views that agree with radical Islam. The *RAND Corp.*, a nonprofit political research firm, said in 2008 that the political party of Erdoğan, the AKP, did not exist before 2001, and won 34% of the vote in 2002 elections, then 46.6% in 2007. AKP is, *"a form of political Islam* [that] *has moved out of the political shadows to become a major actor in Turkish politics"* (*The Rise of Political Islam in Turkey,* Prepared for the Office of the Secretary of Defense, 2008, p. 31)

So it should be no surprise that Turkey did not cooperated with trade sanctions against Iran. In 2012 its trade with Iran was *"as high as USD 100 billion"* (www.presstv.com). Turkey has even stated publicly that it plans to regain its empire! This is important; pay attention to this statement by Turkey's Foreign Minister, Ahmet Davutoglu, in April of 2012:

> "On the historic march of our holy nation, the AK Party signals the birth of a global power and the mission for a new world order. This is the centenary [centennial] of our exit from the Mid-

dle East . . . whatever we lost between 1911 and 1923, whatever lands we withdrew from, from 2011 to 2023 we shall once again meet our brothers in those lands. This is a bounden [morally obligatory] historic mission." (*The Ottomans are back!*, by Burak Bekdil. www.hurriyetdailynews.com, a Turkish news site in English.)

He actually said the empire will return by 2023. The AKP used democracy to gain power but plans to become totalitarian in the future. Erdoğan said, "*Democracy is like a streetcar. You ride it until you arrive at your destination and then you get off*" (*Democracy, Turkey's Double Edged Sword*, by Nicole Dweck, June 10, 2007. The Ground Report, www.ground-report.com).

In March of 2013 an article in *Al Monitor* related comments made by Turkey's Foreign Minister Ahmet Davutoglu, that points to their desire to rebuild their lost empire: "*Without going to war, we will again tie Sarajevo to Damascus, Benghazi to Erzurum and to Batumi.*" (*Davutoglu Invokes Ottomanism As a New Order for Mideast* by Tulin Daloglu. March 10, 2013. www.al-monitor.com /pulse/originals/ 2013/03/ turkey-davutologu-ottoman-new-order-mideast. html)

He suggested an Ottoman model for a new Middle East and North African order. That is another way of saying that they plan to reestablish the Ottoman Empire, which was an association of local rulers, called pashas, under the head of the Ottoman sultans.

On March 29, 2016, *The Clarion Project* website published an article that alleged that Turkey was collaborating with ISIS. It is true that Turkey has arrested ISIS fighters who were planning to attack Jewish children in Istanbul, but documents found by Kurdish YPG fighters, and Syrian Democratic Forces at seven Islamic State locations, show that:

ISIS fighters from all over the world – and particularly from Kazakhstan, Indonesia, and Tajikistan -- were given passage through Turkey to Syria. (*Secrets and Lies: Turkey's Covert Relationship With ISIS*, by Meira Svirsky, www.clarionproject.org)

The article also says that:

ISIS fighters have used the Istanbul and Adana airports and have received permits from the Turkish government to reside in Turkey until they cross over to Syria. (Ibid)

The documents also include bus tickets, electronic Turkish visas, residency permits, and documents with stamps from Turkish immigration officials. This is outright aiding ISIS.

The documents also show *"chemical and explosive materials was transferred from Turkey to Syria."* The article goes on to say that Turkey has given $250-300 million to HAMAS since 2012, and has arranged oil sales for the Islamic State. All of this is known to the U.S. and other nations, but Obama chose to look the other way (I am not surprised).

In 2013 Erdogan visited the 16-acre site of a $100 million mega-mosque, The Turkish American Culture and Civilization Center, being built in Lanham, Maryland which was funded by Turkey.

> "The event was also attended by the leaders of two U.S. Muslim Brotherhood entities." (https://clarionproject.org/turkey-stakes-claim-america-100-million-mega-mosque/)

The Islamic center is the largest in the Western Hemisphere. Erdoğan visited the mosque again when it officially opened, April 2, 2016. There is no doubt that it promotes Erdoğan's Islamist ideas.

> Since taking office in 2003, Erdogan has been implementing his Islamist agenda, slowly but steadily changing Turkey from a secular democracy to an Islamist state: College admissions have been changed to favor religious students, the military has been gutted of its secular generals (with one in five generals currently in prison on dubious charges) and women have been routed out of top government jobs. Honor killings in Turkey increased 1,400 percent between 2002 and 2009. Persecution of artists and journalists has become commonplace as opponents are charged with "crimes" like "denigrating Islam" and "denigrading the state." (Ibid)

Also, Turkey is friendly with the Muslim Brotherhood that had power in Egypt for a short time. Turkey was also the location of the last caliphate, but before then, the caliphate was located in Damascus for hundreds of years. The civil war in Syria is being waged by people who want to restore the caliphate. They are actually calling it a war for the caliphate.

There are several organizations, including ISIS (Islamic State of Iraq and Syria), that are fighting for the caliphate. They claim the reason they are slaughtering Christians is because they are "*purifying the land for Islam*," said Nina Shea, an international human rights lawyer with the Hudson Institute (www.youtube. com/watch?v=B5zz YbB z94I).

We are seeing a dead beast start to open its eyes and move its claws. We are truly approaching the rise of the beast of Revelation from the Abyss.

(4) The Throne of the Beast

In Revelation 2:13 it says the city of Pergamum was where Satan had his throne:

> I know where you live— where Satan has his throne. Yet you remain true to my name. . . . where Satan lives.

The word "throne" (2362) literally means "seat." It was originally a chair in a home where the head of the home would sit. Then at the end of the verse it makes another reference to Satan living there. Most commentaries make reference to the Temple of Zeus that was in the city and many other pagan shrines, but Jesus could be telling us something more.

Jesus could have said something like, "*I know where you live, where there are many idolaters,*" or "*where there are many false gods.*" But instead he said where Satan has his throne. In Rev. 16:10 it says, "*The fifth angel poured out his bowl on the throne of the beast, and his kingdom was plunged into darkness.*" In the Greek it is the same word as above (2362). Pergamum is of course within the national borders of Turkey, and Pergamum means "citadel" which is a fortress. We have already learned how Islam is called a religion of "fortresses" in Daniel 11.

In the original Greek, the word for "dragon" is "drakon" (1404) that can also mean, "serpent." And though it is translated dragon, Revelation tells us clearly that the dragon is in fact the serpent of Genesis; "*that ancient serpent called the devil, or Satan*" (12:9). The main god of Pergamum was Asclepios, who was represented by a serpent. So the first century Christians reading Revelation would have read about a great red dragon, the serpent, Satan, and thought of Asclepios at Pergamum.

Then we read that it is Satan, the serpent, who "*gave the beast his power and his throne*" (13:2). Now, it is easy to read this as saying that Satan caused the beast to have power and the ability to have a throne, or the power to gain a throne. But that is not what it says. In the literal translation it says, "*And the dragon gave its power to it, and its throne, and great authority*" (LIT). *Young's Literal Translation* is even more clear in saying that Satan gave to the beast Satan's own power and Satan's own throne:

> . . . and the dragon did give to it his power, and his throne, and great authority.

And where does Rev. say the throne of Satan is located? Pergamum, also had a serpent on many of its coins (Barclay, *The Revelation of John*, V. 1, p. 99). So here we learn that Satan did not give the beast "a" throne, but "his" throne, which was located in Pergamum. I believe Jesus gave us this information so we will know the location of the throne of the beast. In a book full of symbols and clues, where we are expected to connect the dots to see the picture, it is powerful evidence. There are no coincidences in the book of Revelation, Jesus is telling us where the final beast will live, its political headquarters; therefore, the beast will be a revived Ottoman Empire.

Also, the last word of the verse provides us with even more information, "*where Satan lives.*" In the Greek, the word is katoikeo (2730), and means to dwell "permanently." Both CWD and Strong's agree that it is a permanent or fixed location. There are 7 different Greek words that are all translated "dwell" in the KJV. The word *dwell* or *live* appears 15 times in Revelation; 11 of those times it is 2730. So other Greek words could have been used to tell us where Satan lives, but the word used here tells us it is his permanent home, which means he is still there, in spirit. It is likely that powerful evil spirits reside in the region.

The permanent home of the beast, being in Turkey, does not require that all the former heads of the beast also be headquartered in Turkey. Though we learn about events throughout the past 2,000 years in Revelation, the main focus is the final events shortly before the return of Christ, which is the time of the Great Tribulation. So the main focus of the beast in Revelation is the final 8th head.

I am aware that the actual stones of the temple were dug up and taken to Germany in time for the rise of Hitler, and it likely has much symbolic meaning, but when Jesus spoke the words in Rev. about the location of the throne, it was in Pergamum. And it could yet be returned, because Turkey wants it returned.

(5) Old Prophecies

There are many old prophecies that predict a time when Europe will once again be involved in a massive war, as well as civil wars; likely caused by the many Muslims that have gone to Europe, legally and illegally:

> The fifth period [of Christianity] is one of affliction, desolation, humiliation, and poverty for the Church. Jesus Christ will purify His people through cruel wars, famines, plague, epidemics, and other horrible calamities. He will also afflict and weaken the Latin Church with many heresies. It is a period of defections, calamities, and extermination. Those Christians who survive the sword, plague, and famines, will be few on earth. Nations will fight against nations, and will be desolated by internecine dissensions. (B. Holzhauser, 1850. Yves Dupont, *Catholic Prophecy*, p. 38)

> Are we not to fear, during this period [end time], that the Mohammedans will come again, working out their sinister schemes against the Latin Church? (*Apocalypsis*, B. Holzhauser, 1850; *Trial, Tribulation, and Trumph*, by D.A. Birch, p, 332)

The next passage indicates that Egypt will have a civil war, and ultimately, be ruled over by a very repressive ruler:

> 1 An oracle concerning Egypt: See, the LORD rides on a swift

cloud and is coming to Egypt. The idols of Egypt tremble before him, and the hearts of the Egyptians melt within them. 2 "I will stir up Egyptian against Egyptian-- brother will fight against brother, neighbor against neighbor, city against city, kingdom against kingdom. 3 The Egyptians will lose heart, and I will bring their plans to nothing; they will consult the idols and the spirits of the dead, the mediums and the spiritists. 4 I will hand the Egyptians over to the power of <u>a cruel master, and a fierce king will rule over them</u>," declares the Lord, the LORD Almighty. 5 The waters of the river will dry up, and the riverbed will be parched and dry. . . . 8 The fishermen will groan and lament, all who cast hooks into the Nile; those who throw nets on the water will pine away." (Isaiah 19:1-5, 8)

This prophecy appeared to be fulfilled with the civil war and the rise of the Muslim Brotherhood until they were thrown out of power in 2013. But the Muslim Brotherhood (MB) could gain power once again. If not, then Egypt will likely be invaded after the beast rises out of the Abyss. So whether the MB gains power again, or whether the beast invades, Egypt is destined to suffer under tyranny.

Notice that there is drought and famine during this time or just after the fierce king comes to power. So it appears to take place during the years leading up to or during the Great Tribulation; there will be drought and famine during the GT.

The beast is clawing at the edges of the Abyss, trying to get out; every year that goes by, the beast is getting closer to getting out of the Abyss, and the persecution of Christians increases. While the MB was in power in Egypt, Christians were being attacked and threatened with genocide because they protested against Sharia law and President Morsi's power grab.

And after the military took charge and threw out the Muslim Brotherhood, the persecution got even worse because the MB blamed the Christians for protesting in the streets and ousting Morsi, the MB president. Close to 100 churches have been looted and burned and many Christians were kidnapped, tortured, held for ransom, set on fire, shot, etc. Some of the Christians suffered these persecutions when they refused to convert to Islam, others for just being Christians.

(6) The Glory of Conquest

Imagine the Germans celebrating the murder of 6 million Jews by Hitler. The conquest of Constantinople has been celebrated by the Turks ever since 1453. The numbers pictured below are five-foot tall and stand overlooking the water in Istanbul, celebrating the attack and invasion in 1453.

In 2012, Turkey released a movie glorifying the attack and defeat of Constantinople, called *The Conquest 1453*. It has become a mega blockbuster, breaking records for attendance. The largest English language newspaper in Turkey, *Today's Zaman*, wrote about it:

> "Fetih 1453" (The Conquest 1453), a Turkish spring block buster that glorifies the Ottomans and their conquest of Istanbul, is breaking viewership records in Turkey these days.

> Over 5 million Turks have already seen the movie, making it the country's most popular film of all time. The film's popularity sheds light on Turkey's emerging preoccupation with its Ottoman past: Ottomania is all the rage in Turkey today.

> In recent years, the Turks have re-engaged with their Ottoman past to the point of abandoning the early 20th-century thinking of Mustafa Kemal Atatürk. (www.sundayszaman.com/sunday/newsDetail_getNewsById.Ac tion?newsId= 275971)

You can watch the movie trailers on youtube.com with English subtitles. Just search for "conquest 1453." This film is designed to make the Turks feel good about their past, and to make them desire more of the same glory of conquest. It is basically a propaganda film, like Hitler's propaganda films about the greatness of the Arian race.

"Fetih" means "Conquest."

The surprisingly truthful statement in the movie was when Sultan Mehmed II said he came to conquer Constantinople because the Quran commands it. The biggest lie in the movie was the last scene when the Sultan opened the doors of Hagia Sofia and told all the people who had fled there, that they were free to live and worship as they please; perhaps those not raped, murdered, or sold into slavery. Turkey is good at lying about its murderous past as we saw with the attempted genocide of many Christians during WWI.

The Museum of History in Istanbul, Turkey (Constantinople) shows a display of cannon in front of a large painting of the attack upon the city.

Chapter 6
A Slow Spreading Jihad

(1) Rise of the Muslim Brotherhood

As we have seen, the sixth head of the beast lasted from about 1400 (it started in 1300 but did not start out as an empire, but grew into one) to 1922 when the Ottoman Empire officially became the Republic of Turkey. It was also in 1922 that the office of sultan and caliph were separated. The last ruling sultan was Mehmed VI, who fled Turkey when the office of sultan was eliminated by the Young Turks who were running the government and bringing reforms. The sultan's cousin, Abdul Mejid II, became caliph until the office of caliph was abolished in March 1924. The caliph for Muslims was like the Catholic pope.

The death of the Islamic empire and end of the caliphate energized many people to devote the rest of their lives to the overthrow of Islamic nations that are under the influence of Western powers, and to restore the empire and caliphate. Ibrahim M. Abu -Rabi, author and professor, said:

> Yes, there is no doubt that the disintegration of the Ottoman state -- officially in 1923 -- has had major consequences on Islamic revival, because when Muslim revivalists look at the Ottoman Empire, although it was weak and corrupt, it was a symbol of Islamic unity, not just political unity but theological unity. But there has been a feeling that, since 1924, that unity has disappeared, the Muslim world has had no centre, so to speak. And that, of course, has ushered us into the era of the nation-states in the Muslim world, that are not unified, but as a matter of fact there are different conflicts between them. . . .

(Ibrahim M. Abu-Rabi is a professor at the Duncan Black Mac-donald Center for the Study of Islam and Christian-Muslim Re-lations at Hartford Seminary, Hartford, Connecticut. Author of, *Intellectual Origins of Islamic Resurgence in the Modern Arab World*, Albany: State University of New York Press, 1995). (religioscope.com/info/dossiers/textislam-ism/qutb_ abu-rabi.htm)

Hassan al-Banna Shahid was energized by the loss of the em-pire to form the Muslim Brotherhood (Al Ikhwan Al Muslimun) in Egypt in 1928, with *"five like-minded followers - all of them in their early twenties - to set up the organization to rectify it"* (~~Islamism, fas-cism and terrorism~~, by Marc Erikson. Asia Times, Nov. 5, 2002; www.atimes. com/atimes/ Middle_East/DK05Ak01.html). The Muslim Brotherhood is the mother of many other similar organi-zations throughout the world that have become notorious for their terrorist activities.

The purpose of the Brotherhood and other similar groups is to combat Westernization and secularization of society and ulti-mately to bring all Islamic nations under the rule of Islamic law (Sharia) and the caliph; in other words, another Islamic empire. The first step is to overthrow the governments not under Sharia. The Muslim Brotherhood was responsible for the assassination of the Egyptian King in 1952 and Egyptian President Anwar Sa-dat in 1981. It matters not whether the government is ruled by a dictator with ties to the West, or is a democracy. If it is not ruled by Sharia it must be overthrown.

In 1951 Shaheed Sayyid Qutb, also Egyptian, joined the Brotherhood and became the chief ideologue for Islamic revival-ists worldwide. His most important work, which got him execut-ed, is a book called *Milestones*, also known as *Signposts Along the Road*:

> Sayyid Qutb is easily one of the major architects and "strategists" of contemporary Islamic revival. . . . he gave shape to the ideas and the worldview that has mobilized and motivated millions of Muslims from Malaysia to Michigan to strive to rein-troduce Islamic practices in their lives and alter social and politi-cal institutions so that they reflect Islamic principles. Milestones was written to educate and motivate the potential vanguard of the re-Islamization movement.

. . . In Milestones, he sought to answer some of the fundamental questions such as why Islam needs to be revived? Why no other way of life is adequate? . . . How was Islam established by the Prophet Muhammad (pbuh) and his companions? Can the same method, which was undoubtedly divine in its conception be replicated again? (*A Fresh Look at Sayyid Qutb's Milestones*, by Muqtedar Khan, www.milligazette.com/Archives/01-8-2000/Art4.htm)

How was it originally established? With the sword. Qutb has been called the ideological father of Osama bin Laden. Here is a quote from *Milestones*:

We should immediately eliminate this pagan influence and the heathen [Christian and Jewish and secular] pressure on our world. We must overturn this current society with its culture and leadership of infidels. This is our first priority: to shake and change the foundations of heathens. We must destroy whatever conflicts with true Islam. We should get out from under the bondage of what keeps us from living in the ways that Allah wants us to live. (*Milestones*, quoted in *Islam and Terrorism,* by Mark A. Gabriel, page 118)

Another ideologue of equal influence with Qutb is Mawlana Mawdudi from Pakistan; he states:

Islam is not a normal religion like the other religions in the world, and Muslim nations are not like normal nations. Muslim nations are very special because they have a command from Allah to rule the entire world and to be over every nation in the world. . . . (Ibid, p. 81)

Islam is a revolutionary faith that comes to destroy any government made by man. . . . <u>The goal of Islam is to rule the entire world and submit all of mankind to the faith of Islam</u>. Any nation or power in this world that rises to get in the way of that goal, <u>Islam will fight and destroy</u>. In order for Islam to fulfill that goal, Islam can use every power available every way it can be used to bring worldwide revolution. This is jihad.

. . .The party of God is a group established by Allah himself to take the truth of Islam in one hand and to take the sword in the other hand and destroy the kingdoms of evil and the kingdoms of mankind and to replace them with the Islamic system. This group is going to destroy the false gods and make Allah the only God. (Ibid, page 82)

In *The Missing Commitments,* Muhammad Abed al-Salem says that in earlier times Allah dealt with people through fires and floods, but that he has now given to Muslims the responsibility to torture and kill the enemies of Allah (Ibid, p. 150). But these groups are not the only ones teaching violence and hate; Saudi Arabia is home to a subgroup of Sunnis called Wahhabi. Saudi oil money is being used to build Wahhabi religious schools throughout the world, even in the United States. Wahhabis are teaching Muslims to hate Christians and Jews. Although they live in the United States, they hate us and desire to destroy us and take over the country for Islam.

> "Muslims must kill the enemies of Allah, in every way and eve-rywhere in order to liberate themselves from the grandchildren of the pigs and apes who are educated at the table of the Zion-ists, the Communists, and the Imperialists." (Sheik Omar Abdel Rahman) (*Terrorism and Tyranny: Trampling Freedom, Justice, and Peace to Rid the World of Evil*, James Bovard, p. 32)

Blind Sheik Omar Abdel Rahman was a terrorist leader who died in a U.S. prison in 2017 for his role in the bombing of the World Trade Center in 1993. As soon as the Muslim Brother-hood came to power in Egypt in 2012, President Morsi called for the release of the sheik.

In 2005 the CIA released the contents of a letter that was written by Al Zawahiri, the leader of al-Qaeda in Iraq:

> . . . If our intended goal in this age is the establishment of a cali-phate in the manner of the Prophet and if we expect to establish its state predominantly according to how it appears to us in the heart of the Islamic world, then your efforts and sacrifices, God permitting, are a large step directly towards that goal. (www.washingtonpost.com/wp-srv/world/iraq/zawahiri.10.11.05.pdf)

Apparently, the plan expressed in this letter was to establish the new caliphate in Iraq. The last caliphate was located in Tur-key, but in past centuries it was located in Damascus, Baghdad, Egypt, and Mecca.

The documentary film called, *Where in the World is Osama bin Laden*, interviewed Sheikh al Sweilen, in Saudi Arabia:

Interviewer: Do you think Osama bin Laden caused 9-11?

Sheikh: If one man in a cave was able to do this; what if all Muslims were to resist against America under the leadership of one man?

Interviewer: See, but I don't think that 1.5 billion Muslims think the same way you think.

Sheikh: One single verse from the Quran and they will come.

Interviewer: So why has no one said that verse yet?

Sheikh: These things get planned. Don't disregard it as unlikely. What if we were to burn the refineries just to deprive you of oil?

The Sheikh also acknowledged that many men from Saudi Arabia had gone to fight in jihad against American troops in Iraq. This is why America and its allies can never win a war in Iraq or Afghanistan; there is a continual influx of fighters and money flowing in to fight against the "infidels" from throughout the Muslim world. So Muslims will never run out of money or fighters.

It is not just radical Muslims who are taking part in the movement to revive the empire. Muslims everywhere are being indoctrinated to hate Americans, to hate the British, and to hate Jews and Christians and to desire to kill us in the same way that Germans were indoctrinated by Hitler. Government-run television, radio, and even Friday sermons call for our death and anyone who is connected with us. A Muslim Imam prayed:

O Allah, [give us] one leader to lead jihad for your sake. To liberate the land of Palestine, and the land of Iraq from the Christians. O Allah, the strong and noble one. O Allah, go after the Christians. O Allah, make wars in their homes. O Allah, release your armies upon them. O Allah, make the land of Palestine a graveyard for the Jews. O Allah, make the land of Iraq a graveyard for the Christians. (*Where in the World is Osama bin Ladin?*)

Here are a few more quotes that confirm the lies and indoctrination; a speaker addressed a large crowd and said:

> America is lurking for you, and will not give up until it destroys you completely. Rise up soon because the world is not safe from the hunter [the U.S.] (Iranian video, quoted in *Obsession the Movie*)

> Oh Allah, destroy America. Oh Allah, destroy Britain and its supporters and collaborators. (Dr. Sabri, Mufti of Palestine, Radio Broadcast, Aug. 24, 2001. *Fatal Distraction: The War on Drugs in the Age of Islamic Terror*, by Arnold S. Trebach, p. 278)

> Annihilate the Infidels and the Polytheists! [the Christians] Your [Allah's] enemies are the enemies of the religion! Allah, disperse their gathering and break up their unity, and turn on them, the evil adversities. Allah, count them and kill them to the last one, and don't leave even one. (Prayer by Suleiman Al-Satari, Palestinian Authority TV, July 8, 2005. www.front page-mag.com)

This sort of call to kill Jews and Christians has been going on for a long time; we have only recently paid attention because of 9-11 and other terrorist attacks. Here is another from 1944 that was spoken by the Mufti of Jerusalem:

> Arabs, rise as one man and fight for your sacred rights. Kill the Jews wherever you find them. This pleases Allah, history, and religion. This saves your honor. Allah is with you. (Moshe Pearlman. *Mufti of Jerusalem: The Story of Haj Amin el Husseini*, (V. Gollancz, 1947, page 51)

In 2004, a Muslim cleric spoke to a large crowd:

> Very soon, Allah willing, Rome will be conquered, just like Constantinople was. . . . this capital of theirs will be an advanced post for the Islamic conquests, which will spread through Europe in its entirety, then will turn to the two Americas, and even Eastern Europe. (Yunis Al-Astal, Hamas MP & Cleric. 4-13-08. Memritv.org, #1739)

Was the huge crowd a bunch of radical terrorists? No, it was thousands of normal Muslims from around the world who were in Mecca for the annual hajj pilgrimage. This is more proof that the terrorists are just the ones who are acting on what the Imams are calling ALL the Muslims to do.

They have come up with all sorts of crazy lies, designed to incite hate and the desire to kill us. In the next quote, Hussam Abu Al-Bukhari relates information published in an Islamic book:

> Since we are talking about America, we should consider how it came into being. America was founded through the genocide of the indigenous people of North America, South America, and Australia. American civilization was founded only <u>after their complete annihilation</u>. . . . They <u>killed hundreds of millions</u>. An entire chapter in this book is devoted to the eating of the flesh of the Indians. It is an entire chapter on <u>how the Americans, or the British immigrants, who were referred to as "pilgrims", would kill the Indians and then eat them</u>; cooked, barbequed, made into kebabs, you name it. . . . There were books explaining how to eat human flesh. (March 4, 2013. Reported on Memritv.org #3763) (About a book titled, *America: The Cultural Genocides*, by Dr. Akash.)

If you are not educated on this issue, everything he said was a complete lie. The total population of the natives in the Americas was only several million; and every native was not murdered, and English cannibalism is total fiction. They use whatever they can to speak against America, Israel, and Europe. Also spreading throughout the Muslim world is the lie that the U.S. wants to destroy Islam, and that its invasion of Iraq is proof:

> America is causing all the trouble in the world. I heard that they want to eradicate Islam. (*Where in the World is Osama bin Laden?*)

They claim the CIA brought down the World Trade Center in order to have an excuse to invade Iraq and Afghanistan, because it is a war against Islam. (Well, the CIA may have known about it and turned the other way, and may have even put explosives in the towers to increase the destruction, but not because it wants a war with Islam.) They use this lie to gain recruits to radical Islamic organizations such as the Party of Liberation, also known as Hizb ut-Tahrir, or HT. HT exists to liberate Islam from Western domination, and to prevent America and Western European nations from destroying Islam, but is aimed mostly at the U.S.

The organization calls on members to attack the U.S. on all fronts, then establish an Islamic super-state, and then global ji-had, but especially to destroy America. One of its videos begins with; *"Since the destruction of the Khilafah* [caliphate], *the Muslim Ummah has faced constant oppression."* The organization holds conferences around the world, produces slick videos, and even has a full color magazine. They are outlawed in England but are allowed to spread their message in the U.S.!

At this writing the Organization of the Islamic Conference is making a serious effort to get an international law passed at the United Nations to make it an international crime to speak against Islam or try to convert a Muslim to Christianity. Known as Resolution 16/18, it would make it illegal to criticize Islam or tell the truth about its history. Obama pressed for its passage in the United States, but it was rejected. Expect to see more efforts like this as Muslims work together for the common cause of global dominance.

Ayaan Hirsi Ali was born in Somalia but fled to Holland to escape tribal and Islamic oppression as a woman in Islam. She became a social worker and member of parliament where she campaigns for women's rights, but she is now speaking on behalf of Christians who are being murdered in ever-increasing numbers throughout the Muslim world. She said in a *Newsweek* article:

> In recent years the violent oppression of Christian minorities has become the norm in Muslim-majority nations stretching from West Africa and the Middle East to South Asia and Oceania. In some countries it is governments and their agents that have burned churches and imprisoned parishioners. In others, rebel groups and vigilantes have taken matters into their own hands, murdering Christians and driving them from regions where their roots go back centuries. (Ayaan Hirsi Ali: *The Global War on Christians in the Muslim World*, by Ayaan Hirsi Ali, The Daily Beast.com (Newsweek), Feb 6, 2012)

Christians are being burned, hacked to death, beheaded, mutilated, shot, and stabbed, while their churches and homes are bombed and burned. This is caused by the growing militancy of many Muslims who are no longer content to live side by side with Christians, but demand that they convert or die. The fundamentalist Muslims see the Christians as standing in the way of Islamic Law in their country, so they are trying to kill all the Christians or cause them to flee into other countries. And it all started with the Muslim Brotherhood. This is all part of the rise of the beast of Revelation 13.

(2) Civilization Jihad

One of the methods of Islamic expansion was by settlement. Muslim merchants were at one time some the most successful in all of Africa and Asia, which is the primary way in which Islam spread beyond the reach of the armies of conquest. The merchants moved their families to establish a presence in a city; then their numbers gradually grew until they were able to coerce the local government to make concessions to them, and even coerce them into converting, least the merchants take their ships and go to another port.

This infiltration is sometimes called *civilization jihad*, whereby Islam gradually infiltrates a whole society. They are now being very successful in Europe, UK, and Canada. They are also doing their best to infiltrate America, having already elected representatives at the national and state levels.

Dr. Sami Alrabaa is a professor of Sociology and an Arab/ Muslim culture specialist. He taught at Kuwait University, King Saud University in Saudi Arabia, and then Michigan State University before moving to Germany. He is now an ex-Muslim. In a column in the *Canada Free Press*, Dr. Sami Alrabaa wrote about Geert Wilder's prosecution in Europe for so-called hate speech against Islam and exposed some of the actual hate speech of Muslims against nonMuslims. Geert Wilder was prosecuted for telling the truth about Islam and the motives of Muslims living in Europe, which is to gradually take over. Here is part of that article published January, 31, 2009 (reprinted by permission):

> . . . There is an abundance of fatwas (religious edicts) by Muslim authorities inciting to genocide and suicide attacks against Christians and Jews. All these fatwas are based on the Koran and Hadeeth.

> Ali Gom'a, the grand mufti of Egypt, the highest Muslim religious authority in the world, supports murdering non-Muslims. In the daily Al Ahram (April 7, 2008), he says, "Muslims must kill non-believers wherever they are unless they convert to Islam." He also compares non-Muslims to apes and pigs, not only the Jews.

> Muhammad Sayyid Al Tantawi, president of Al Azhar University also approves of killing and maiming Christians, Jews, and other infidels. He added, "This is not my personal view. This what the Shari'a Law says, the law of Allah, the only valid law on the earth."

> Yousef Al Qaradhawi, the spiritual leader of the fundamentalist organization, the Muslim Brothers, urged on Al Jazeera TV (Jan. 9, 2009) Muslims to kill the Jews, not only in Israel but also worldwide. He added, *No peace can be made between us (Muslims) and the non-believers. This what our holy book says. This what Allah says.*"

> Saudi Arabia's Grand Mufti, Sheikh Abdulaziz Bin Abdullah Bin Mohammed al Sheikh said on Iqra' TV channel, "Killing [TV] producers who show women unveiled is legal."

> The Saudi Sheikh Saleh Al-Lehadan, head of the Supreme Judiciary Council, told Al Watan daily, (March 25, 2008) "After getting rid of the Jews in our Arab land, we must turn to the Christians. They have three options: either they convert to Islam, or leave, or pay Jizia (protection taxes). . . ."

> Most recently, demonstrators in Berlin and Munich, and elsewhere in Germany, raised banners reading, "Hamas! Hamas! Jews to the gas". The police did not arrest anyone of them and nobody filed a court case against them for inciting to murder which in the German law is punishable. . . . Wilders' comparison of the Koran to Adolf Hitler's "Mein Kampf" and describing it as a fascist book is not inappropriate. Hitler referred to the Jews as "rats and vermin" and the Koran and fascist Muslims call the

Jews "The descendants of apes and pigs".

It is not Wilders who should be prosecuted, but people like Gom's, Al Qaradhawi and their peers. They must be brought to justice before the International Tribunal. Inciting to genocide is an egregious crime.

Many Westerners are intimidated by fascist Muslims and that is what the latter want to achieve at the end of the day. . . . His message is very clear: "Westerners, wake up before it is too late." . . .

Tarek Ramadan visited the Islamic Center in Bilelefeld, Germany (May 21, 2008) and gave a speech. Before he began his speech, he asked if there were any journalists in audience. As the answer was negative, he said, "OK, now I feel free to say what I really want." Ramadan is well-known for telling his infidel audience something and his Muslim audience another thing.

Ramadan said, "My brothers and sisters, we must exploit the so-called democracy and freedom of speech here in the West to reach our goals. Our Prophet Muhammad, peace be upon him, and the Koran teach us that we must use every conceivable means and opportunity to defeat the enemies of Allah. Tell the infidels in public, we respect your laws and your constitutions, which we Muslims believe that these are as worthless as the paper they are written on. The only law we must respect and apply is the Shari's."

Ramadan added, "The Germans claim that they want to integrate you in their society. We tell them we are going to integrate them in our Umma (Muslim world) after converting them to Islam." . . . (*Wilders Prosecution is a Welcome Opportunity to Expose Islam*, Dr. Sami Alrabaa.)

The reason I have to provide so many quotes and details, exposing the truth behind Islam, is because you are not hearing about this on your TV network evening news; because those left-wing journalists are ignoring the negative news about Islam. You are also not hearing this in most churches, because of the incorrect teaching on Revelation, such as the Pre-Trib Rapture and even that there is no such thing as the beast of Revelation and Antichrist that will come, so many churches are asleep to this threat.

MUSLIMS ATTACK CHRISTIANS
Catholic celebration attacked in France
World's population hits 7 billion   7:59 PM ET

This is a screenshot of a news story in 2011 that reported Muslims throwing rocks at Christians in France during a Catholic celebration. This will be coming to a city near you, as soon as the population of Muslims grows large enough.

A 45-year-old British citizen of Derby, was attacked by a group of Muslims and severely beaten to unconscious, because he had a cross hanging from his rearview mirror.

> "I fled from Pakistan to escape violence such as this, but more and more the same violence is coming into Britain." (www.derby telegraph .co.uk/news/derby-news/attack-outside-littleover-restaurant-leaves-662302)

News reports such as this are a daily occurrence in UK and EU, but found only on certain websites and outlets, not the large networks. The EU is run by far left liberals that are blindly destroying Europe. They are forcing the EU member nations to accept millions of Muslim migrants into their nations, removing crosses from public buildings and even from pictures because Muslims cry that they are offended by the crosses, even canceling Christian celebrations, and removing Christianity from Europe's history. They ordered Slovakia to *"redesign its commemorative coins by eliminating the Christian Saints Cyril and Methonius."** Slowly but surely EU is being taken over by Islam.

Being forced to accept millions of migrants is one of the reasons that the UK voted to leave the EU in 2016, but it appears to be too late, it has already been taken over by Islam because it is not only illegal to criticize Islam in Britain, but you cannot even say anything that Muslims do not like. People are being arrested for speaking the truth about Islam. London even elected a Muslim mayor in 2016.

Poland and a few other Eastern European countries are refusing to allow the importation of millions of Muslims. They have had nationwide marches against the EU migration policy, with crowds so large it looked like the entire nation participated. So the EU is threatening Poland and other nations with economic sanctions. Hungary's Prime Minister said they, *"will not give in to blackmail from Brussels and we reject the mandatory relocation quota."* * (The EU threatens Poland for not accepting Muslim refugees, Jun 19, 2017, www.theblaze.com/news/2017/06/19/the-eu-threatens-poland-for-not-accepting-muslim-refugees-heres-how-they-responded/)

An anti-immigration protest in Poland in 2015.

(2) Muslim Brotherhood's Plan for America

It is not only the stated mission of the Muslim Brotherhood (MB) to establish a caliphate and another Islamic empire, it is also their stated mission to conquer Europe and North America by civilization jihad, because they do not have the military ability to confront us at the present time.

When the Ottoman Empire was defeated and Turkey became a secular state, most of the Muslim world also entered the modern age. You can find photos of Afghanistan, Iran, and Egypt in the 1950s that show women working in offices dressed in the same clothing as Europe or the U.S. In photos, the female graduates of Islamic universities were not wearing the hijab, even into the 1970s. But slowly, in the 80s and 90s, an increasing number of women were wearing the hijab in graduation photos. Then in the 2000s 90% or more are wearing the hijab.

This shows the gradually increasing influence of the MB throughout the Muslim world. They are probably the most powerful nongovernmental Islamic organization that has ever existed in the Muslim world, and their power is continually growing.

The influence of the Muslim Brotherhood is global; they are in at least 100 nations, either overtly or covertly. There are some seventy-plus organizations which the MB started or funds, or is otherwise connected with, which are all living out the agenda of the MB. These include dozens of Islamic organizations here in the U.S. Below is a *"Friends of the Muslim Brotherhood"* list from a 1991 document (other organizations have been formed since this list was created, such as CAIR, the Council on American and Islamic Relations, which is also connected to HAMAS):

* ISNA = Islamic Society of North America
* MSA = Muslim Students' Association
* MCA = The Muslim Communities Association
* AMSS = The Association of Muslim Social Scientists
* AMSE = The Association of Muslim Scientists and Engineers
* IMA = Islamic Medical Association
* ITC = Islamic Teaching Center

* NAIT= North American Islamic Trust
* FID= Foundation For International Development
* IHC= Islamic Housing Cooperative
* ICD= Islamic Centers Division
* ATP= American Trust Publications
* ISNA = Islamic Circle of North America
* IBS= Islamic Book Service
* MBA= Muslim Businessmen Association
* MYNA= Muslim Youth of North America
* IFC= ISNA FIQH Committee
* IPAC= ISNA Political Awareness Committee
* IED= Islamic Education Department
* MAYA = Muslim Arab Youth Association
* IIC = Islamic Information Center
* IAP = Islamic Association For Palestine
* UASR = United Association For Studies And Research
* OLF = Occupied Land Fund
* MIA = Mercy International Association
* IIIT = International Institute for Islamic Thought

(Taken from, *An Explanatory Memorandum, On the General Strategic Goal for the Group* [Muslim Brotherhood], *In North America,* 5/22/1991 www.Investigativeproject.org /documents/ misc/20.pdf, p. 32, in Arabic and English; and www.pjtv.com/?cmd=mpg& mpid=387)

Here is some truly shocking information, right from the horse's mouth, from the above referenced document, the chapter titled: *The Process of Settlement,* sections 4 & 5. Section 4, *Understanding the role of the Muslim Brother in North America*:

> The process of settlement is a "Civilization-Jihadist Process" . . . The Ikhwan [Brotherhood] must understand that their work in America is a kind of grand Jihad in eliminating and destroying the Western civilization from within and "sabotaging" its miserable house by their hands and the hands of the believers so that it is eliminated and Allah's religion is made victorious over all other religions. Without this level of understanding, we are not up to this challenge and have not prepared ourselves for Jihad yet. It

is a Muslim's destiny to perform Jihad and work wherever he is and wherever he lands until the final hour comes, and there is no escape from that destiny except for those who chose to slack. But, would the slackers and the Mujahedeen be equal.

5- Understanding that we cannot perform the settlement mission by ourselves or away from people:

A mission as significant and as huge as the settlement mission needs magnificent and exhausting efforts. With their capabilities, human, financial and scientific resources, the Ikhwan will not be able to carry out this mission alone or away from people and he who believes that is wrong, and Allah knows best. As for the role of the Ikhwan, it is the initiative, pioneering, leadership, raising the banner and pushing people in that direction. They are then to work to employ, direct and unify Muslims' efforts and powers for this process. In order to do that, we must possess a mastery of the art of "coalitions", the art of "absorption" and the principles of "cooperation".

Middle East expert and author, Mike D. Evans, gives some analysis of the above document:

The document describes the "process of settlement" as the approved means of gaining a foothold and, eventually, control of the United States. A better phrase might be "deceptive peaceful assimilation". The memorandum advises Muslims that, in order to be successful, they must follow six basic and progressive steps to preparing for successful jihad in the US. It is the same approach that the MB is using in all countries. Their success is becoming visible in Europe already. (Article title: *The Muslim Brotherhood's Plan for America*, www.middleeast media-group.com : tinyurl.com/aqlodfx)

Here are those basic steps of infusing Islam into the world:

1. Establish an effective and stable Islamic Movement led by the Muslim Brotherhood.
2. Adopt Muslim causes domestically and globally.
3. Expand the observant Muslim base.
4. Unify and direct Muslims' efforts.
5. Present Islam as a civilization alternative.
6. Support the establishment of the global Islamic State, wherever it is. (Ibid)

Here are three quotes from "peaceful" Muslims here in the U.S. who are connected to the Muslim Brotherhood:

Islam isn't in America to be equal to any other faith, but to become dominant. The Koran should be the highest authority in America, and Islam the only accepted religion on earth." (Hamas-linked CAIR cofounder and longtime Board chairman Omar Ahmad, 1998) (www.jihadwatch.org/2012/01/we-reject-the-un-reject.html)

"We reject the U.N., reject America, reject all law and order. Don't lobby Congress or protest because we don't recognize Congress. The only relationship you should have with America is to topple it. . . . Eventually there will be a Muslim in the White House dictating the laws of Shariah." (Muhammad Faheed, Muslim Students Association meeting, Queensborough Community College, 2003)

"If we are practicing Muslims, we are above the law of the land." (Mustafa Carroll, executive director of the Dallas-Fort Worth CAIR branch, 2013. www.frontpagemag.com/2013/dgreen field/dallas-cair-director-muslims-are-above-the-law-of-the-land/)

The pledge of the Muslim Student's Association, a Brotherhood organization, says:

Allah is my lord,
Islam is my life,
The Koran is my guide,
The Sunna is my practice,
Jihad is my spirit,
Righteousness is my character,
and Paradise is my goal.
I enjoin what is right,
I forbid what is wrong,
I will fight against oppression,
and I will die to establish Islam.

Righteousness to most Muslims is enforcing their Sharia law, and oppression refers to any laws that hinder the practice and spread of Sharia law. The pledge is very similar to the MB pledge:

Allah is our objective.
The prophet is our leader.
Qur'an is our law.
Jihad is our way.
Dying in the way of Allah is our highest hope.

The U.S. federal government was infused with MB friendly people during the Obama administration and their actions continue; because once certain policies and procedures are put into play they are hard to reverse. Thus, the U.S. federal government is cooperating with many MB-connected organizations helping by them spread their lies that Islam is a religion of peace, and that Muslims in North America are moderate and not interested in conquering America or Canada or Europe. Books have been written detailing how Muslims have infiltrated government agencies, such as *Stealth Jihad: How Radical Islam is Subverting America without Guns or Bombs*, by Robert Spencer, and *Stop the Islamization of America: A Practical Guide to the Resistance*, by Pamala Geller.

Muslims are also making many converts in our prisons and in the black community. They have also made many friends and alliances within the political left and even some in the conservative right. This has resulted in Muslims with connections to the Muslim Brotherhood getting jobs of influence in Washington, even in the White House under Bush, but especially with Obama. These Muslims work to stop criticism of Islam, and work against Israel. When they appear on TV they deny that they want Sharia in America, but then promote it privately.

In late 2012 an Egyptian magazine actually boasted that the MB had 6 members who had infiltrated to high levels within the U.S. government, as reported by World Net Daily:

[A]n Egyptian magazine claims six American Muslim leaders who work with the Obama administration are Muslim Brotherhood operatives who have significant influence on U.S. policy.

Egypt's Rose El-Youssef magazine, in a Dec. 22 story, said the

six men turned the White House "from a position hostile to Islamic groups and organizations in the world to the largest and
most important supporter of the Muslim Brotherhood." (www.wnd.com/2013/01/egyptian-mag-affirms-brother-
hood-infiltration-of-white-house/#GaJxFEJsFCgTR0oV.99)

The MB got its inspiration from the fundamentalist Islamic
Wahabbism found in Saudi Arabia; so it is no surprise that millions of dollars from Saudi Arabia are being used to fund many
of the above-mentioned MB organizations. Saudi money also
funds Middle East study departments at many of our universities
which teach only good things about Islam, and hate for Israel
and even the United States. Here is a small list:

* 20 million dollars for a Middle East study department at the U.
of Arkansas
* 5 million to Berkley's Middle East study department
* 22.5 million to Harvard U.
* 28.1 million to Georgetown U.
* 11 million to Cornell U.
* 5 million to MIT
* 1.5 million to Texas A&M
* 1 million to Princeton
* 5 million Rutgers
* 5 million to Columbia

Millions of dollars have gone to UC Santa Barbara, John
Hopkin's, Rice, U. of Chicago, USC, UCLA, Duke, Saracuse,
Howard, and many more. These Middle East study departments
hire Muslim professors which brainwash the students into believing that America is evil, and Israel is murdering helpless Palestin-
ians without cause.

The money does not appear to be coming from the Saudi royal family because they do not seem to act like religious extrem-
ists. Their main interests are making money and living like play-
boys, just like typical billionaires on Wall Street, and own large
amounts of stock in many companies around the world; nonethe-

less the money is coming from somewhere in the country. Perhaps the government gives the religious leaders a certain number of billions each year and they decide where it goes.

If all the above were not enough, the Turkish American Coalition is working to infiltrate America through our Native American Tribes, giving them scholarships to attend college in Turkey, sending dozens of tribal leaders on all-expense-paid trips to Turkey, and getting the tribes to bring Turkish companies into the U.S. to set up bases on tribal land outside the jurisdiction of the federal government. We have good reason to believe their motives are suspect because of what they have already done in Uzbekistan. Here is some revealing information from an article that broke this story at pjmedia.com:

> Evidence from Uzbekistan points to a possible nefarious motive: Infiltration and Islamization. The government of Uzbekistan is claiming that private Turkish business interests in the Central Asian country have been acting as a front for banned Islamist extremists. According to Agence France-Presse:
>
>> [The Uzbek government is] accusing Turkish companies of creating a shadow economy, using double accounting and propagating nationalistic and extremist ideology. ... Long wary of the influence of Islamic fundamentalism ... secular authorities appear to be linking Turkish private business to the activities of the Nurcus, an Islamic group that is banned in the country. [Nurcus is also banned in Russia].
>
> Is it really in America's national security interests to have thousands of Turkish contractors and their families flooding into America's heartland and settling in semi-autonomous zones out of the reach of American authorities? Especially if their intent is to form intimate business and social ties with a long-aggrieved minority group? (pjmedia.com/blog/stunner-turkey-infiltrating-native-american-tribes)

Congress is even working to make all this happen, which shows how ignorant they are about the real agenda behind Islamic global expansion. The MB has said that either they succeed now or in a hundred years, *"But this country* [U.S.A.] *will become a Muslim country"* (Abdulrahman Alamoudi, Islamic Association of Palestine Conference, Chicago, Il, 1996. The Center for Security Policy, 2010.)

A former Muslim who still lives among them and knows all the inside information has revealed some interesting facts on this subject of civilization jihad. This is what they believe:

We will fight the infidel to death, but until then:

* American laws will protect us.
* Democrats and Leftist will support us.
* N.G.O.s will legitimize us.
* C.A.I.R. will incubate us.
* The A.C.L.U. will empower us.
* Western Universities will educate us.
* Mosques will shelter us
* O.P.E.C. will finance us
* Hollywood will love us.
* Kofi Annan and most of the United Nations will cover our asses.

(www.siotw.org/modules/news_english/item.php?itemid=777)

Most Christians in America are well educated about the anti-christian organization, the ACLU, that works hard to remove crosses, manger scenes, the Ten Commandments, and Christian free speech in public places, but what you don't know is that the organization has, at this writing, eight Muslim lawyers who are no doubt very zealous at attacking Christianity every way they possibly can, while defending Islam.

Muslims are not just here in America because they like the weather, they are here to take over the country like they have done in other countries, and are doing now in France and other EU nations. And the Muslim Brotherhood is the main organization behind the majority of all the Islamic organizations in America.

For more information on Islam and the Muslim Brotherhood in America, I recommend you watch videos on youtube.com such as, *The Grand Deception,* or read the book, *The Muslim Mafia*, by P. David Gaubatz and Paul Sperry or other good books. Visit *American Congress for Truth*, www.americancongressfortruth.com. Also help fight against the influence of Islam in American life and government with political action by joining *ACT! for America*; www. actforamerica.org.

The latest news about the Muslim Brotherhood in America is that they have formed a political party:

> The Muslim Brotherhood is launching a political party in America for the purpose of electing Muslims and influencing legislation that is favorable to Islam. This development should come as no surprise: the number of mosques in the United States has escalated 74 percent since 2000. (*Muslim Brotherhood Launches Political Party in America,* by Jim Denison, April 9, 2014 www.christianheadlines.com, and http://news.investors.com)

> *"Islam is not a* (constitutionally-protected) *'religion.' Islam is a totalitarian expansionist, militaristic, seditious political system."* (Ann Barnhart, political and economic commentator)

Is this information beginning to look like a global conspiracy to gradually take over the world? This information makes the popular book series, *Left Behind*, by Jerry Jenkins and Tim LaHaye, seem like fiction, oh wait, it is fiction! But the MB plan for global jihad is not a dream we will wake up from, it is a nightmare we are going to fight through. Many Christians are going to die, but we should take heart because we know that the beast will only wage war for 42 months, and then Christ returns.

Chapter 7
The False Prophet

(1) The Islamic Religion

The second beast in Rev. chapter 13 does not get as much attention as the first beast. This second one is not an empire like the first, because it is the religion of the empire-beast. Notice that it has two horns:

> Then I saw another beast, coming out of the earth. He had two horns <u>like a lamb,</u> but he <u>spoke like a dragon.</u> 12 He exercised all the authority of the first beast on his behalf, and made the earth and its inhabitants worship the first beast, whose fatal wound had been healed. (Rev. 13:11-12)

It is no accident that the second beast is like a "lamb" because it claims to be a lamb religion, a religion of peace. The second beast professes to be a lamb, but it acts like a dragon and speaks like a dragon because it was the religion of more than one head of the  beast and will be the religion of the final head. The history of Islam shows that it does not bring peace, but only death and destruction. Even when nations are ruled by Islamic law and Islam is the dominate religion, the nations are plagued with murder, rape, slavery, and corruption. The word "assassin" originated within Islam, because of a group of Muslims who frequently engaged in murdering their opponents.

The two horns represent the two main divisions of Islam, Sunni and Shiite (Shia). Is it a mere coincidence that inside the Muslim holy temple in Mecca, the Kaaba, hangs a ram's head with two horns?

> The horns of the ram that Abraham had slaughtered (in place of Isaac or Ishmael) were hanging on the wall facing the entrance. . . . (Azraqi, 1858, p. 106. Quoted in *The Hajj*, F.E. Peters; p. 12)

The second beast is said to exercise *"all the authority of the first beast on his behalf."* In other words, it works on behalf of the empire beast because the goal of Islam is to dominate the world politically and religiously. These two beasts, political and religious, work together for the same cause, to rule the world.

The first beast, empire, comes out of the sea; this probably refers to the Mediterranean Sea because the beast represents empires that have existed next to the Mediterranean. But the second beast comes out of the earth. Is there any place more descriptive of earth than Arabia, which is mostly dirt and sand? Arabia is where Islam began.

In other chapters of Revelation this second beast is called *"the false prophet"* (Rev. 16:13, 19:20, 20:10). Muslims refer to Muhammad as *"Muhammad the Prophet"* or just *"the Prophet."* There have been many false prophets in the world but how many of them officially had "the Prophet" as part of their title? None as infamous as Muhammad.

(2) Miraculous Signs

> "And he performed great and <u>miraculous signs,</u> even causing fire to come down from heaven to earth in full view of men. 14 <u>Because of the signs</u> he was given power to do on behalf of the first beast, <u>he deceived the inhabitants of the earth.</u>" (13:13-14a)

I will explain verse 14 then 13. The Greek for *"miraculous signs"* is (semeion) (4592) and means *"miracle, sign, token, wonder"* (Strong). The Quran, in Arabic, is hailed as being the greatest lyrical poetical work that could ever be written, especially by a man supposedly illiterate, which is why the Quran itself is called a miracle. And the verses of the Quran are actually called *"miraculous signs."*

. . . the miracle of the "Ayates", a word generally rendered "Verses", but really meaning "<u>miraculous signs</u>" of the Qur`an. (Dinet, *The Life of Mohammad: Prophet of Aallah,*, p. 70)

So the Arabic word for "~~verses~~" of the Quran actually means "~~miraculous signs.~~" And the *Islamic Dictionary* website says, "*Proof, evidence, verse (from the Quran), lesson, sign, revelation, miracle etc.*" (www.islamic-dictionary.com). Therefore, the above verse in Rev. 13 refers to the Quran. The Quran says:

We will soon show them <u>Our signs</u> in the Universe and in their own souls, until it will become quite clear to them that it is the truth. . . . (41:53) (Shakir)

A book written on the supposed miracles of Muhammad, says:

Truly, the Quran will remain the greatest Miracle . . . (*Miracles of the Messenger*, Dar-us-Salam Research Division, Darussalam Publishers & Distributors, 2004, page 17)

Revelation says, "*Because of the signs . . . he deceived the inhabitants of the earth,*" that is, Arabia. It was because of the verses which Muhammad spoke from time to time that many of the early converts became believers:

As for the Arab of the Hijaz, comprehending the most subtle hints of the language of the Quran his own language and who welcomed the Surahs as they issued from the lips of his fellow countryman: the genial, inspired messenger of Allah, that listener was overwhelmed by such sudden surprise that he remained as if petrified. Could this <u>supernatural language</u> come from Mohammad, known to be completely illiterate and possessing no other knowledge than that due to nature and intuition? This seem [ed] completely impossible. . . . the <u>irresistible effect produced by the recitation of the Quran</u> . . . (Ibid, p. 71-72)

Hearing the verses recited in such amazing poetical style convinced the simple Arabs and tribesmen that the words had to be from heaven, and that Muhammad was a true prophet. It is truly amazing how specific and accurate are all the chapters of the book of Revelation, but especially in this important chapter!

(3) Causing Fire to Come Down From Heaven

We just learned that the miraculous signs are actually the verses of the Quran, but the fire does *appear* to be literal:

> 13 And he performed great and miraculous signs, even causing fire to come down from heaven to earth in full view of men. (Rev. 13:13)

Many people believe this verse refers to an actual miracle that will deceive people into following the Antichrist, like when Elijah called down fire upon the alter of Baal, but it is symbolism. Notice that it actually does not say that the second beast *calls* fire down like Elijah did, but that it *causes* fire to come down. The Greek word is poieo (4160) and means:

> To make, form, produce, bring about, cause, spoken of any external act as manifested in the production of something tangible, corporeal, obvious to the senses, completed action. (CWD)

Thus, most translations say that the beast "makes" fire to come down from heaven. So this is not a fake miracle like most Bible commentaries suppose, it is something very real. It says that the beast actually produces or creates some kind of actual fire, and it is fire that can be seen; so to be mentioned in the Bible, and be part of the real world, I believe it refers to nuclear fire.

It is significant that Revelation does not say that the beast with ten horns makes fire come down, which is to use nuclear weapons, though it will use nukes during WW 3. Revelation is saying here that the beast with two horns, which is the Islamic religion, will make the fire, which <u>could</u> refer to Muslims using a stolen nuke or homemade bomb even before the ten-horned beast rises to power.

There are several verses of the Quran that tell Muslims to use fire to destroy non-believers and the enemies of Allah:

> Those who reject our Signs, We shall soon cast into <u>the Fire</u>: as often as their skins are roasted through, We shall change them for fresh skins, that they may taste the penalty: for Allah is Exalted in Power, Wise. (4:56) (Ali)

This verse says Muslims will burn the skin off those who refuse to convert to Islam, and then the victims will be given new skin so it too can be burned off, again and again. What a peaceful religion! Who would not want to be part of this religion? LOL

The next verse below is a clear threat against Christians because they are accused of adding the Holy Spirit and Jesus to the Godhead. Then the second verse below it is a threat against Jews:

> Soon shall We cast terror into the hearts of the Unbelievers, for that they joined companions with Allah, for which He had sent no authority: their abode will be the Fire: And evil is the home of the wrong-doers. (3:151) (Ali translation)

> Allah hath heard the taunt of those who say: "Truly, Allah is indigent and we are rich!" - We shall certainly record their word and (their act) of slaying the prophets in defiance of right, and We shall say: "Taste ye the penalty of the Scorching Fire!" (3:181) (Ali)

The Quran also speaks of fire upon infidels on the Day of Judgment:

> Our Lord, Thou wilt certainly assemble mankind together on the Day about which there is no doubt . . (As for) those who disbelieve, surely neither their wealth nor their children shall avail them in the least against Allah, and these it is who are the fuel of the fire. (3:9-10) (Shakir)

We seem to be getting a lot of fire, and the fire is not divine fire from heaven, but fire generated by the Muslims. Read this verse carefully:

> Surely we have prepared for the unbelievers chains and shackles and a burning fire. (76:4) (Shakir)

There are many more verses like these that some Muslim leaders may say are telling them to use nuclear weapons on nonbelievers. Therefore, one or more nuclear weapons could be used against Israel or America even before the start of World War 3.

If the Muslim Brotherhood, or other terrorist group, succeeds in using a nuclear weapon against America, it will cause many more Muslims to join their fight. It will make them believe they could actually succeed and they will say that Allah has allowed them to be successful in using the nuclear weapon(s). When the twin towers of the World Trade Center collapsed, the whole Muslim world celebrated. Should an American city get nuked before WW3, it will become a holiday. It will be a victory that will make them boast and celebrate. It may also help unite the Muslim world.

However, it may simply refer to the fact that the beast will rely upon the texts of the Quran for justification for its use of nuclear weapons during WW3, because it is the religion of Islam that is telling them to take this action and use fire to destroy the unbelievers.

(4) Worship the Beast

> 4 People worshiped the dragon because he had given authority to the beast, and they also worshiped the beast and asked, "Who is like the beast? Who can wage war against it?" (Rev. 13:4)

The Greek word for worshiping the beast is proskuneo (4352), which literally means to bow down before someone. The *Complete Word Study Dictionary* says:

> In the NT, generally, to do reverence or homage to someone, usually by kneeling or prostrating oneself before him. (CWD)

Every instance of the word "worship" in the book of Revelation is proskuneo. Bowing before someone was considered a form of worship. I don't think it was a coincidence that John used that word when he could have used one of several different Greek words such as "sebomai" (4576) which means:

> To revere, stressing the feeling of awe or devotion, to worship religiously. To stand in awe of someone, to reverence, venerate, worship. (CWD)

"Sebomai" appears several times in the New Testament, such as in Matt. 15:9, Mark 7:7, and five times in Acts. So it is likely that proskuneo is used in Revelation to point us to the way Muslims pray, by bowing down to the ground. Of course John did not know that a future religion would require bowing on the ground, but the Holy Spirit did.

(5) Image of the Beast

There is not going to be an ugly beast with seven heads standing behind a microphone, *"Earthlings, I command you to worship me!"* Since the beast with seven heads is not literal, and the beast with two horns is not literal, then we should not expect the image to be literal. There is not going to be an image of the Antichrist set up in a rebuilt Jewish Temple, and it is not a computer or artificial intelligence!

> He deceives those who dwell on the earth by the signs which he was granted to do in the presence of the beast, <u>telling those who dwell on the earth to make an image </u>to the beast who was wounded by a sword and lived. 15 He was allowed to give <u>breath</u> to the image of the beast, that the image of the beast should both speak and cause as many as would not worship the image of the beast to be killed. (Rev.13:14b-15) MEV

Did you notice that the image is given breath? The Greek for "breath" is pneuma (4151) and is the same word used in Rev. 11:11 where it says, *"a breath of life from God entered them, and they stood on their feet."* It means "spirit" or actual breath. A computer can speak but it will never have breath, or life. So it is important to note that the text plainly tells us that the image can speak and has breath like a living being.

Now, <u>notice that people are commanded by the image itself to worship itself or be killed</u>. This is important. Nowhere does it say that people must take the mark of the beast or be killed; people are not even required to worship the first beast or the second beast or be killed, but <u>they must worship the image or be killed</u>. The image is said to have actual breath and can speak and cause people to be killed if they refuse to worship it; so, what is the image?

The Greek for image is eikon (1504), and denotes a reproduction or representation of the original, such as a reflection on the water or the statue of a man. In 2 Cor. 4:4 it says that Christ is *"the image of God"* and uses the very same Greek word for "image."

So the image does not have to be an object, but can be a person. This image breathes air and requires people to worship it, therefore, it must be a human being. It does not say an image is made "of" the beast; most translations say an image is made *"to the beast,"* which is why a few translations say *"in honor of."*

Keep in mind that the image is made *to the first beast*, which is an empire; it is not an image to the second beast, and it is human. This image is a reproduction or representation of the first beast, so there must be some part of the empire that is remade or represented in the image, which is human. Once again we must study history to find the answer.

We have already learned that the invading Arabic armies gave Christians and Jews three choices: convert to Islam, submit to Islamic rule, or fight. If they fought and lost, the men of fighting age were murdered, the city plundered, and many women and children were raped and sold into slavery. So the Muslim armies traveled from city to city and demanded people submit to them or face death. The future revived Islamic empire will also have armies that do the same.

Notice that the image will exercise *"all the authority of the first beast on his behalf."* Therefore, the armies will have the authority to act on behalf of the Revived Ottoman Empire. So the armies of the beast will be representatives of the empire, that is, representations or images of the empire beast.

So the image to the beast is the Islamic armies of conquest that will go from city to city, or nation to nation and demand that people submit to them or die. Therefore, to worship the image is to submit to Islamic armies. If you convert to Islam, then that is not merely worshiping the image, that is totally giving over to the beast and false prophet, which is taking the mark of the beast, more on that shortly. Worshiping the image is submitting to Islamic rule.

> "If anyone worships the beast and its image and receives its mark on their forehead or on their hand, 10 they, too, will drink

the wine of God's fury, which has been poured full strength into the cup of his wrath." (Rev. 14:9b-10a)

We are told several times that God does not want us to worship the beast, or the image of the beast, and since those who submit to Islamic rule are worshipping the image, then this means that God wants all cities and nations to fight, never submit. This is the last war, and Islam teaches that when the Islamic Jesus returns to Earth he will destroy Christianity; therefore, it is very likely that after a city or nation submits and lays down their weapons, they will then be required to convert or die. So it is better to fight than to lay down your weapons thinking that you will be allowed to live as subject peoples, only to discover that it is no longer acceptable to merely submit. Some Christians may choose to not submit and not fight back, and just be slaughtered. The Bible says *blessed are they that die in the Lord from now on* (Rev. 14:13).

Remember, the meaning of the Greek for "worship" was not religious devotion or veneration, but *"reverence or homage to someone, usually by kneeling or prostrating oneself before him"* (CWD). That is a very good definition and picture of submitting yourself to someone more powerful, which is what the Muslim armies once demanded and will demand again. God does not want us to worship the beast, or the image of the beast, which is to submit ourselves to the Islamic soldiers.

However, the astute Bible student may notice that it was not the first beast who commanded the image to be made, but the second beast. The second beast gives it life. It is Islam that calls for holy war, or Jihad. It is the Islamic holy books of the Quran and Hadith that speak of Jihad and command people to engage in Jihad. Islam will be the motivating force behind the Islamic armies of conquest. It is Islam that calls for the creation of the armies of holy war.

(6) Image of Satan

You may have heard this talked about on TV or youtube videos, but if you have not, here is some shocking information. On the outside of the Dome of the Rock are some marble slabs. This marble has naturally occurring images that appear to be the face of Satan complete with horns. Here are two different pictures of the same slab of rock:

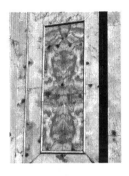 

But, you can just ignore that, I expect to see a man walking around with 666 stamped on his forehead, LOL, no don't ignore it.

I had to steal these pictures from youtube videos. If someone has been there and can send me a high resolution picture, I will send you free copy of this book, after update.

Chapter 8
The Mark, Name, & Number of the Beast

(1) The Mark of the Beast

> 16 <u>He</u> also forced everyone, small and great, rich and poor, free and slave, to receive <u>a mark on his right hand or on his forehead</u>, 17 so that no one could buy or sell unless he had the mark, which is the name of the beast or the number of his name. 18 This calls for wisdom. If anyone has insight, let him <u>calculate</u> the <u>number</u> of the beast, for it is man's number. His number is 666. (Rev. 13:16-18)

The first thing to notice is that this verse is in the second half of Rev. 13 where it refers to the second beast. Anytime it refers to the first beast, it makes an appropriate reference; as we saw above, it says, "***He*** *exercised all the authority of the* <u>*first beast*</u> *on his behalf*. . ." So when it refers to "he" in the last half of Rev. 13, it refers to the second beast unless otherwise noted.

Then we go on down to where it starts talking about the mark and it starts with, "<u>*He also*</u> *forced everyone . . . to receive a mark.*" Again, it does NOT say that the mark is of the first beast, therefore, it is the mark of the second beast. Since it is the mark of the second beast, it is not the mark of any global government; even if the first beast were going to rule the entire world, but it will not. It is the <u>mark of the false prophet, Muhammad</u>, or the <u>mark of Islam</u>.

Most translations of the above verses do a little bit of interpreting based on assumptions, rather than just translating. Thus most Bible versions say you cannot buy or sell unless you have the mark, "<u>*which is* the name of the beast <u>*or*</u> the number of his name.*"

Is the mark going to be the name of the beast or the number of his name? Didn't John know which it was? John was not confused; it is the translations that are confused. Let's look at the literal translation:

> . . . not any could buy or sell, except the one having the mark, or the name of the beast, or the number of its name. (LIT)

Notice where the first comma is located. This is also the way it reads in the KJV, MEV, and NKJV:

> 17 so that no one may buy or sell, except he who has the mark or the name of the beast or the number of his name. (KJV)

That little word "or" is in the Greek text, both times, and it means "or." So it literally says that you cannot buy or sell unless you have <u>any one of three things</u>:

1. the mark of the beast or
2. the name of the beast or
3. the number of the name of the beast

Having any one of those three will allow you to buy or sell. So this is powerful evidence that it refers to being a follower of the second beast, because if you have the name of the beast, then it signifies that you believe in him; the same with the number of the name of the beast, or the mark.

All of these point to the second beast, but because of mistranslation, we have merged these three and the mark of the beast has now become the number of the beast, 666! This is WRONG. This means, that even if you don't take the mark of the beast, you could still be allowed to buy or sell if you have the name of the beast. So what is the difference between the three?

The right hand is important in the Bible; for example, Jesus is seen sitting at the right hand of God. *The Complete Word Study Dictionary* says:

> Concerning the mark being on the right hand, God is said to be at the right hand of the person whom He helps as the enemy is to the right of him whom he seeks to overcome and the accuser to the right of the accused. By the right hand the whole man is claimed, whether in action or in suffering ... (CWD, p. 405)

Since the *right hand* has meaning beyond the literal sense, it does not require a literal mark be placed on the right hand or forehead. The right hand holds even more importance in Islam. Muslims receive reward in the right hand, but punishment in the left hand; the right hand is the hand of honor or cleanness, but the left is dishonor or uncleanness (Q. 69:19-26). One verse in the Quran refers to the Muslim people as a whole as *"those of the right hand"* (Q. 56:90-91).

The Greek for "mark" is charagma (5480) and means, *"An engraving, something graven or sculptured, an impression, mark or symbol."* (CWD). Thayer's Greek Definitions adds cattle brand to the definition. *Word Meanings in The New Testament,* says:

> The noun charagma comes from the verb charasso, "to engrave." So it means <u>a stamp or impress</u> made on an object. . . . It was evidently some kind of an <u>official seal</u> impressed firmly on the right hand or forehead. Imperial seals of that period have been found. (by Ralph Earle, p. 465)

John Gill's Exposition of the Entire Bible says:

> Maimonides says, it was a custom with the Gentiles to mark themselves with their idols, showing that they were their bought servants, and were marked for their service.

It was also common to mark a slave, or even a soldier, with a brand. Thus Strong's says, *"a badge of servitude."* A synonym of this word is "seal" (sphragis 4973), defined as, *"mark, seal, impression."* The difference between these two words, charagma (5480), and sphragis (4973), seems to be found in the idea of protection being also connected with sphragis, as being sealed up in a jar, or a scroll being sealed. Thus it could not be opened by the messenger without the recipient seeing that it had been opened.

So we see that the 144,000 in Rev. 7 have the seal, or mark (sphragis), of God in their foreheads and are protected from harm (Rev. 9:4), but those who take the mark (charagma) of the beast are not protected but will receive God's judgment. The two words are similar in meaning, therefore, the word *charagma* (5480) could have been translated "seal," as in a royal seal, as we saw in the definitions above.

The seal (sphragis) of God in Rev. 7, which is placed on the foreheads of the 144,000, is clearly not a literal mark that can be seen; therefore, the mark or seal (charagma) of the beast does not have to be a literal mark.

The meaning could have multiple levels of application, so on one level it could be symbolic and refer to ownership, which would merely refer to converting to Islam. Therefore, taking the mark signifies that you belong to Islam. Being on the forehead would symbolize being in the person's mind, and being in the right hand would signify taking hold of; in other words, converting to Islam.

But there could also be a literal mark, but it will not be a global account number; the number is not the mark! Those with the mark, name, or number are followers of the beast. These three things will point us to the identity of the first and second beasts.

Even though it is not a global account number that is placed on the forehead or right hand, there are a lot of connections to a mark, both literally and figuratively, within Islam. We learned that the meaning of the word "mark" can refer to something carved or engraved, such as an official seal of a ruler. In ages past a ruler would put some melted wax or ink onto the bottom of a letter and then press his seal/stamp/mark onto it, thus making it official.

So we should not be surprised that Muhammad had a literal seal/ stamp/ mark that he used on his official documents. He sent letters to neighboring nations calling on them to join Islam or be invaded, and put his stamp/ seal/ or mark at the bottom of each letter:

Seal of Muhammad;
Seal / Mark of the Beast?

As best I can determine, the words on the seal say something like, *"Allah/ Messenger/ Mohammad,"* and is short for *"Mohammad is the messenger of Allah."* In 2019 I found a website that says it does in fact say this.

This appears to be a shortened version of the *Shahadah*, which is the Islamic statement of faith; *"There is no God but Allah, and Muhammad is his messenger."* This is all one needs to say to become a Muslim. In other words, to accept Muhammad's mark is to become a Muslim. Is Muhammad's seal the literal mark of the beast? ISIS fighters in Iraq have been seen wearing this on their foreheads.

Muhammad's seal has made its way onto a black flag that is supposedly a reproduction of one that Muhammad used while doing jihad. The words at the top of the flag are the Shahadah. It was seen in Libya and Syria and now Iraq, and is carried by ISIS. It has also been seen being attached to the windows of cars in Michigan where there is a large Muslim population.

There is another connection that Islam has to a mark or seal. In the Quran, Muhammad is called *"the seal of the prophets"* (33:40). The Arabic word for "seal" is khátam , (خاتَم)and means *"an official mark (seal)"* (*Muhammad: The Seal of the Prophets*, Dr. Muhammad Abra-

ham Khan, p. 161). Even though most Islamic scholars teach that it has the meaning of "last" because the seal or signature was put at the end of a letter, in classical Arabic, the root for khátam *"clearly points toward the idea of the placing of an impression of a signet -ring upon something, that is, the idea of a 'seal'* (Wahiduddin Richard Shelquist, wahiduddin.net/ words/khatam.htm, see also the Arabic-English Lexicon, by Edward W. Lane, p. 702). So even the Arabic word for "seal" has a meaning similar to the Greek word used in Rev. 13, and the Quran calls Muhammad a seal/mark of prophets.

So a seal, sign, or mark is directly connected to Muhammad in several ways. Keep in mind that symbolism is never an exact match to the thing symbolized; a close resemblance or connection is all that is necessary, and Revelation is 99% symbolism (see Book 1 for a full definition of symbolism).

But there is more; Muhammad says in the Quran that his people have a mark on their foreheads. When Muslims bow in prayer they press their foreheads and hands onto their prayer rugs so that when they raise up they have marks on their foreheads and hands, thus they have three visible impressions on their skin (the forehead and both hands). Most translations of the Quran say, *"Their marks are on their faces in consequence of prostration"* (48.29) (Maulana Ali); the Pickthal translation says, *"The mark of them is on their foreheads from the traces of their prostration."* So are the impressions from bowing in prayer the mark of the beast?

According to a book titled, *IRAN: Desperate for God*, published by *Voice of the Martyrs*, some Muslims are so fervent in prayer that they actually cause a callus to form on their foreheads. (A callus is a thick area of rough skin.) This callus is considered a "sign" of holiness.

So Islam is literally connected to mark/seal/stamp in several ways. Keep in mind that there is also a name of the beast and number of the name. So the mark of the beast is separate from the name and number of the name.

You can see by the above information that a meaning can be multilayered, that one symbol can have several different applications, or the thing symbolized can mean several different related things. For example, to Christians the symbol of an anchor means faith and hope, but can also mean being secured in the storms of life, rather than being tossed by the waves. You can see how the meanings are similar yet different, and yet they point to the exact same symbol, the anchor. We see this here in Revelation.

Next is the name of beast, which is the name of the second beast, not the name of the first beast. We know the name of the second beast; it is Islam, sometimes spelled Islaam. So what do you suppose it would mean if you were to "take the name of the beast"? It would mean that you convert to Islam. So now we will move on to number three, the number of the name of the beast.

(2) The Number of the Name of the Beast, 666

As we saw above, the mark has symbolic meaning, yet there could be a literal mark, therefore, the number is likely going to be symbolic and literal, because we are told to figure it out. But, you may say the mark is supposed to be a number. No, we have seen that the mark of the beast is only a mark, and the name of the beast is the name of the beast; it is not the same as the number of the name of the beast. About the number *Barnes Notes* states:

> The phrase "the number of the beast" means, that somehow this number was so connected with the beast, or would so represent its name or character, that the "beast" would be identified by its proper application.

The number 666 is a symbolic number that points us to who the beast and his followers are, which is why the Bible tells us to "calculate" the number, or literally to figure it out. Therefore, I believe we can now know the number, at least we can figure out the symbolic part of it.

Since we now know that the number 666 will not literally be stamped on people's foreheads, it must contain symbolism designed to point us to the identity of the second beast. There is no limit to the interpretations of the number of the name. You can find 666 in the names of dozens of famous people, past and present, supposedly including Al Gore, William Jefferson Clinton, Henry Kissinger, and the Pope. To understand the number of the name of the beast we must first look in the Bible, and then to history.

An occurrence of 666 is connected to Israel's enemies:

> The weight of the gold that Solomon received yearly was 666 talents, <u>not including</u> the revenues from merchants and traders

and from all the <u>Arabian kings</u> and the governors of the land. (1 Kings 10:14-15)

Since this passage clearly shows that Solomon received far more than 666 talents of gold, there must be significance in the use of 666 in this passage. Solomon collected revenue in various forms of taxes, called tribute, from the neighboring countries. So this passage connects 666 with the nations that surround Israel. This is one of only three passages in the Old Testament where 666 directly occurs, and the word *Arabia* appears here as well. The Arabians are stated as being Israel's enemies in 2 Chronicles 21:16, and 26:7, and they still are today. And Arabia is where Islam began.

The number appears indirectly several times, such as in the story of David and Goliath. Goliath stood 6 cubits and a span tall, his iron spearhead weighed 600 shekels, and he had 6 different types of armor and weapons: a helmet, a coat of mail, bronze leg protectors, a javelin, a spear, and a sword. An assistant carried his shield, so Goliath personally had only six different weapons and armor. What is the significance of this? Here symbolic 666 is connected with those who were waging war against Israel. Who have been the greatest enemies of both Jews and Christians for over 1,400 years? The Muslims. Who desires above all else to wage a literal war against Israel and all Christians? Muslims.

Goliath started the attack, but David killed him by using a stone (with God's help of course); so in the future, Muslims will wage the final world war but God will destroy them with a literal stone from heaven, which is an asteroid impact (these events are discussed in detail in Book 4 about the Wrath of God).

The number of the name of the beast is also in Daniel 2 where the king erected a solid gold statue that was 60 cubits tall, 6 cubits wide, and the people were commanded to bow down and worship it at the sound of 6 instruments: horn, flute, zither, lyre, harp, and pipes. The sound of the musical instruments called people to bow down to the image; Muslims are called to bow down in prayer five times a day at the sound of a person calling out words in a manner that sounds like singing. Music was used during Ottoman attacks, such as before and during the battles against Constantinople:

> This night they worked [preparing for the battle] in high excitement, shouting and singing, while fifes and trumpets, pipes and lutes encouraged them on. . . .

> All along the line of the walls the Turks rushed in to the attack, screaming their battle-cries, while drums and trumpets and fifes urged them on. (*The Fall of Constantinople 1453*, S. Runciman, Cambridge U. Press, p. 126-127, 133)

The Babylonians threatened to kill anyone who did not bow to the image. Millions of people who have refused to bow toward Mecca in prayer have been killed, and many more will yet be killed.

The book of Ezekiel says, *"In the sixth year, in the sixth month on the fifth day"* (8:1), Ezekiel had a vision. In this vision he saw six men approaching *"each with a deadly weapon in his hand"* (9:2). A seventh man put the mark of God on the foreheads of all the righteous. All those without the mark were killed by the 6 men; in the 6th year and 6th month (666). Here the mark / seal of God is associated with those who are righteous and all persons without the mark are killed in God's judgment. This is similar to what happens in Revelation, those with the mark of God, the 144,000, are protected, but those without it, because they have the mark of the beast, will be killed in the Wrath of God. The six men do the killing, and the followers of the beast will do the killing during WW3.

Similar connections with 666 are found in modern Israel. Jerusalem was a divided city until 1967, with half the city controlled by the Arabs. Then in June, the 6th month, several Arab nations mobilized their armies for war against Israel, so Israel attacked first, and the war lasted 6 days (which is why it is called the Six Day War). This gives us three 6s (666). Also, it was officially declared over at 6 pm local time in Jerusalem. Israel won the Arab half of Jerusalem and a large piece of Jordanian-controlled land. So this is another thing that connects 666 with the surrounding nations, who are Islamic, and were fighting against Israel.

It was on the 6th day of that war that the Israelis gained control of the Temple Mount where stands the Dome of the Rock (the Jews immediately returned control to the Muslims).

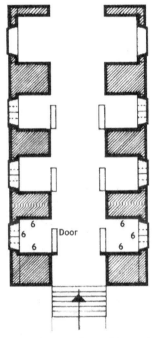

East Gate of the Temple

A powerful reference to the number 666 is found in Ezekiel's description of a future Jewish Temple. Whether real or symbolic, there is an astonishing mention of 666:

> 10 Inside the east gate were three alcoves on each side; the three had the same measurements . . . 12 . . . and the alcoves were six cubits square. (Ezekiel 40:10, 12)

Here we have six alcoves, or niches, and each are six cubits square, which is 6x6x6. (Other translations do not plainly say they are square, but all books and drawings I consulted had these alcoves being square, because if the right wall is 6 cubits then the left wall must also be 6 cubits unless the room is really messed up architecturally.) So, what this presents to us is, that each person walking through the east gate is <u>surrounded by six alcoves, each representing 666</u>! This is another passage that tells us who the people of 666 are; those who surround Israel. Could it be any clearer?

The above is powerful evidence. The Bible does not include this information to take up space. It was put there for our benefit, to provide us with information we need to know.

Some people object to finding 666 in the manner above, but since the number is symbolic, and we are told to figure it out, then we can expect to see it this way. Otherwise, it must be literal, but that is nonsense. If it were literal, then it would not have told us to figure it out. There are other references to 666 in the Old Testament that are less discernible and less certain, so I will not include them here.

All the above evidence tells us that the enemies of God today are the people that surround Israel, which are all Islamic nations, and identifies them as the people of the beast and false prophet, not the fictional world government of the EU or the UN. Islam is the greatest enemy of freedom and justice the world has ever known. Muslims openly declare their plan to take over the world, and they will get their chance during the Great Tribulation.

(3) The Number 6 in Islam

We have seen that 666 refers to the enemies of God in the Bible, which are Muslims, but does the number 6 or 666 have any direct connection with Islam? Since you are never going to find 666 stamped on anything actually connected to the second beast, it is connected in the form of multiple occurrences of the number 6.

We learned that the mark and number of the beast are associated with the second beast, not the first beast, and we find that the number 6 is associated with Islam in many different ways. Muslims go to mosques on Friday, the 6th day of the week; there are 6 volumes of the Hadith or Traditions, which are the collected sayings of Muhammad outside of the Quran. And there are also 6 articles of faith:

* Belief in Allah	* Belief in prophets
* Belief in angels	* Belief in the day of judgment
* Belief in Quran	* Belief in predestination

Islam began just over 600 years after the birth of Christ, Muhammad died in 632 at the age of 61 (or 62) (666); and if Christ died in 32 A.D., as many scholars believe, then Mohammed died only a couple of months off from being exactly 600 years later.

The first significant battle, and one of the most important battles fought between the Arabs and the Eastern Roman Empire, was in 636, at Yarmuk, (notice that Yarmuk has 6 letters). It was important because the victory opened up all of Syria and Palestine to the Muslims. The Muslims trapped the Romans, so the Romans agreed to lay down their arms and surrender, but once the weapons were gathered up, the Romans were all slaughtered:

> The Battle of the Yarmuk, the slaughter in that gorge of Syria, was decisive; it was perhaps the most decisive battle in the history of the world. . . . Very often in history it has been so; one decisive action has changed in a day the political future of a whole country, even of a whole civilization . . . (*The Battle Ground: Syria and Palestine: The Seedplot of Religion*, Hilaire Bellock, p. 243)

Also, the Battle of Yarmuk lasted 6 days (*Yarmuk AD 636: The Muslim conquest of Syria*, by David Nicolle, page 77).

The Muslim general, Amr, who invaded and conquered Egypt, also has 666 associated with him:

> There is some discrepancy among the Arab authorities on the subject of 'Amr's age at the time of his death, though their agreement upon the date of that event is nearly unanimous. It may be taken for granted that he died on the Yum al Fitr A.H. 43, corresponding to January 6, 664. (*The Arab Invasion of Egypt*, by Alfred Butler, p. 546)

Sultan Mehmed VI (6th), was the last sultan of the Ottoman Empire. Sultan has <u>6</u> letters, Mehmed has <u>6</u> letters, plus <u>6</u>th, gives 666. For an added bonus, he was also the 36th ruling Ottoman sultan.

The number 666 is also associated with modern Muslims

who are working to bring back the Islamic empire. Hassan al-Banna Shahid and five others (a total of 6 persons) founded the Muslim Brotherhood (MB), often just referred to as the Brotherhood or Ikhwan in Arabic. Notice also that Hassan, Shahid, and Ikhwan all have 6 letters. Plus, Shahid was born in 1906.

Shaheed Sayyid Qutb, the writer of MB propaganda, was also born in 1906; he was executed in 1966, and Sayyid has 6 letters. And more recently, Abu Musab al-Zarqawi was a terrorist leader in Iraq after the U.S. invaded in 2003. He was killed by U.S. forces 06/2006, and he was born in 1966. Are all these occurrences just a coincidence? Perhaps.

In June of 1996, while American troops were in Saudi Arabia, Muslims exploded a suicide truck bomb that destroyed Khobar Towers, which was the housing complex for U.S. troops in Dhahran. Notice that it took place in June, the 6th month, of 1996, and "Khobar" and "Towers" each have 6 letters.

Finally, when the Ottoman Empire became modern Turkey, President Atatürk presented "Six Arrows" of reform. The National Security Council of Turkey has 6 members, and "Turkey" has 6 letters, the capital of Turkey is "Ankara" which has 6 letters. More coincidence?

God made the world in 6 days and mankind is supposed to work 6 days and rest the 7th day. So the number 6 is connected with man and work, but also to man's efforts at saving himself in the form of a false religion of effort or striving; Islam is nothing but a religion of striving. It is all outward effort, bowing and reciting memorized prayers a certain number of times, and fighting wars.

Someone posted a question online about the number of verses in the Quran and it was answered by someone who knew a lot about the subject. Here is that question and answer that explains the number of verses in the Quran:

****

Question:

How many verses (Ayahs) are there in the Quran? People mention different numbers about the amount of the Quranic verses. If so,

why? Are there different types of Quran? Is addition or deletion of
the verses in question? Can you explain it?

Answer:

Scholars have different opinions about the number of the
Quranic verses. But this conflict is just about "numerating" the verses. All the scholars are in agreement about the content and originali-
ty of Quran. . . .

Here are some points about the difference:

Some scholars numerated the long sentences as two or three
verses, while some others regarded them as one whole verse.

Besides, Shafii scholars regarded "basmala" (1) as a part of each
sura and didn't numerate them. But the Hanafi scholars regarded
each Basmala as specific verses, so counted them. . . .

The number of the verses according to Scholars:

Ibn-i Abbas (ra): 6616,

Nafi (ra): 6217,

Shayba (ra): 6214,

Scholars of Egypt (ra): 6226,

Zamahshari (ra) (the genius Eloquence Scholar of the Arabic
language and literature); 6666.

Bediuzzaman, mujaddid (the reformer) of the 13.century, also
has the opinion of 6666 verses.

Ibn-i Huzeyme, one of the big imams, made the following expla-
nations on "6666" issue while handling the "Quran's miracle of
number" topic of his book titled "An Nasih wa'l Mansuh":

There are 1000 verses about promising (wa'ad);

1000 about threat (wa'id);

1000 command (amr) verses;

1000 forbiddance (nahy) verses;

1000 information and story verses;

1000 warning and example verses;

500 verses about ruling;

100 verses about invocation and glorification;

66 "nasih and mansuh" ("the abrogating and abrogated") verses.

Totally there are 6666 verses in the Quran.

Consequently, the expression "Quran has 6666 verses," is based
on the mentioned points.

But today, accepting the opinion of Kufa, all Qurans consist of

6236 verses. . . . (askaquestionto.us/question-answer/revealedbook/
how-many-verses-ayahs-are-there-in-the-quran)

****

WOW! You can see from the above information that at least three respected Islamic scholars used Qurans with 6666 verses, and at least one with 6616 verses. This explains why some Christians claim that the Quran has 6666 verses, and even many Muslims believe it has, because some of them do! I checked the four physical Quran translations that I own, and some online, and they all had 6236 verses.

So why do most of the Qurans we use today have only 6236? In all probability, at some point in the past few hundred years they decided to stop using the Qurans with 6666 verses and 6616 verses. This means they purposely chose to use some very long verses rather than divide them into more readable and reference-able shorter verses, most likely because they realized that Christians were associating the Quran with the number of the beast 666.

In addition to the verses, there are 114 chapters, called suras. If you count or calculate the number of the second beast, like we are told to do, then: 1+1+4=6.

You saw the ten-horned mosque in Saudi Arabia in another chapter; there are 3 mosques in Turkey that each have 6 minarets (666)?

Sultan Ahmed Mosque

1. The Mugdat Mosque in Mersin, with a height of 266 feet.
2. The Sabanci Mosque in Adana, built 1998.

3. The Sultan Ahmed Mosque, also called the Blue Mosque, in Istanbul, built 1609-1616.

You may be asking, how many minarets do other mosques have? It is *not* standard to put six minarets on a mosque. Some have one, but most have either two or four. While I am here, the word "mosque" has 6 letters.

Lastly, but certainly not least, is the numerical value of "Allah." I found several Islamic websites that clearly say that the numerical value of "Allah" is 66. In Arabic (al-+'ilāh, the god) (www.the freedictionary.com); notice that it has 6 letters in Arabic. And even in English *Allah* is sometimes spelled *Allaah* and *Islam* sometimes spelled *Islaam*, with 6 letters (www.fatwa-online.com/aboutis laam/0020224_03.htm) (www.indotalisman .com/99names. html, www.deenislam.co.uk/ Sufic-introduction tothe99Names.pdf, www.discoveringislam.org/ yah weh_in_ quran. htm).

The *Coptic Apocalypse of Pseudo-Athanasius* (ca. 715), whether a real or fake prophecy, tells us what people believed about the Muslims of that day:

> First, that nation [Islam] will destroy the gold on which there is the image of the cross of the Lord our God in order to make all the countries under its rule mint their own gold with the name of the beast written on it, the number of whose name is 666. Afterwards they will count the men and write their names in their documents, and set upon them high taxes. . . . (*Seeing Islam as Others Saw It*, R. Hoyland, p. 283-284)

Notice the claim that the name of Muhammad equals 666. A book published in 1713 said:

> The numeral letters in Mahomet's name make 666, as Montague observes in his Appello Casarem [Appeal to Caesar]; and so does Napier reckon. (John Floyer, *The Sibylline Oracles,* page, 324. Page 172 in the new edition of the book, *The Sibylline Oracles: Revised and Updated,* 2011.)

The book, *I Appeal to Caesar,* by Richard Montague, was published in 1625 and is currently not available in Google Books to learn how the author arrived at 666.

I will not give the background of how Allah is connected to the moon god and Baal. Other people have already done that in books and online. Though interesting, it does not add to the proof that Islam is the religion of the beast and false prophet, so I do not cover it here.

We know that the mark and number of the beast are not of the first beast, but of the second beast, which is Islam. So the number of the name of the beast most likely refers to the many occurrences of the number 6 that is connected to Islam.

Now, that being said and proven above, there is yet something clsc which is very interesting, to say the least. It is the appearance of the word Allah. In Hebrew, each letter has a number, so the "w" in Hebrew has the value of 6. Here is an image of the word Allah in Arabic:

Can you see the two w's? *Yea, that's just a coincidence.*

If you noticed the black flag, there were almost 3 Ws on it. So now let us look at a modern font of the Shahadah:

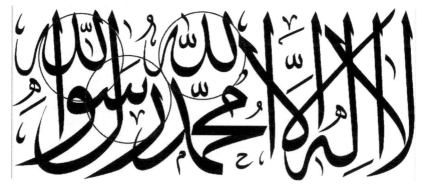

Notice that there are 3 large Ws in the circles, and the the circle on the right has 2 small Ws with it, so there are a total of 7 Ws in the

Shahada unless you don't count the one that looks like an E laying down, in which case there are 6 ws; or six 6s using Hebrew gematria.

(4) A New Theory About the Mark is Proven Wrong

Walid Shoebat, author of *God's War on Terror*, grew up speaking and reading Arabic, so he believed he saw something in the Greek text that most of us could never see, which is that the Greek letters *chi xi sigma*, which signify 600 60 and 6, look very much like the Arabic word, *Bismillah* that means, *"in the name of Allah,"* along with crossed swords, which is found in many Islamic emblems and flags. He believes that John actually saw the Islamic word and the crossed swords and tried to copy it; so what we see as being 666 in the Greek is not that at all. However, there is plenty of evidence that this theory is very wrong.

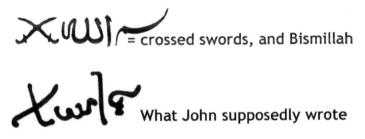

= crossed swords, and Bismillah

What John supposedly wrote

Shoebat says the top half of the image is what John saw, and that John actually wrote down something like the bottom part. He says that scribes thought he had written the number 666 as seen in the Codex Vaticanus, seen here:

This new theory has taken off on many websites and youtube.com; even well-known Bible teacher Chuck Missler has taught it, but it is not accurate for several reasons. First, notice that the scribes would have had to turn the middle squiggle 90 degrees and move the line from beside it to above it. And then also turn the middle letter. That is major editing, not merely writing letters that resembled what John wrote.

Since the early Bibles were handwritten, it is probable that only a few copies of the Bible would resemble *Bismillah* and crossed swords. If Shoebat were to have seen a different manuscript, he would not have seen anything that looked like *Bismillah*.

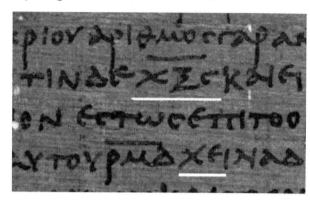

This image is from the *Chester Beatty Papyri* collection. The letters that look like an X and E are Greek letters that appear frequently in Greek documents.

Notice the letters above the white line. They don't look very much like crossed swords and Bismillah. Look at the bottom line, there is another X and E with a line after it; is that another failed attempt to write *Bismillah?*

Shoebat references the Vaticanus codex found in the Vatican library, but it was not complete, and was pieced together. The book of Revelation was missing, so they added a much later copy of Revelation to make a complete Bible. So Revelation in Vaticanus is not so ancient, but later. Another codex, the Sinaiticus, has 666 written out in words and in capital letters, which do not in any way resemble *Bismillah* or crossed swords! It was a very common practice to write the Bible in all capital letters.

Which was in the original text that John wrote? Was it 666, or the words *six hundred, sixty, six*? We will not know this before the return of Christ, but it makes no difference insofar as this issue is concerned.

However, a piece of evidence does exist that points to the words being written out originally. Notice the line above the letters in the *Chester Beatty Papyri* above. That line above the text is not part of the numbers, it is a scribal mark that means that the numbers below it are an abbreviation. I do not believe that John would have put that mark there if he wrote numbers originally.

To me this means that the number was originally written out in words, *six hundred sixty and six.* Then a later scribe changed it to numbers and put the "abbreviated" mark above it. You don't put the "abbreviated" mark above something that was not changed by a scribe.

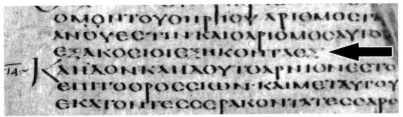

This codex has 666 in words, not numbers. The arrow points to the line. Notice the number "14" on the left. That begins chapter 14.

But <u>more importantly, the text actually says it is a number</u>. The word "number" appears four times in the last two verses, *"for it is man's number. His number is _____"* So John was not trying to write something other than a number. Everything John wrote down, he either saw in a vision, or is what an angel told him during the visions; he did not write down impressions or assumptions that a scribe mistook for a number, and <u>he says it is a number</u>!

But even if he wrote the number, perhaps God intended it to point to *Bismillah*? No, that is not possible because the verse says it is a number. It also says that we should "count" the number of the beast. How can you count up or calculate something that is not a number?

This inaccurate interpretation includes much twisting of the meaning of the original Greek text in order to smooth out the conflicts. Shoebat and his followers are doing this in an attempt to make the passage make sense with *Bismillah*. So they have contrived alternate meanings for "count" and "number" and end up making the verse say something very different.

They claim an alternate meaning for "number" (arithmos) (706), is "multitude," and they use "determine" instead of "count," so they come up with this; *"let him that hath understanding <u>determine</u> the <u>multitude</u> of men belonging to the beast: for it is a <u>mul-</u>*

titude of men; and his multitude is (crossed swords, Bismillah)."

They are using the word "multitude" incorrectly, as though it were not connected to arithmos. Using "multitude" this way is dead wrong. Here is what *Thayer's* Greek dictionary says about arithmos:

> 1) a fixed and definite number 2) an indefinite number, a multitude

The word "multitude" as used in the above definition refers to a large number, not a specific group of anything, certainly not a group of people. The way Shoebat and his followers are using it, it refers to a group, the group being the Muslims.

The word "multitude" from the Greek *arithmos* can be used only if its use retains the original meaning. As in, *"he has a multitude of problems."* Notice that the sentence could have been worded this way; *"he has a large number of problems."* So it retains the meaning connected to "number." But as it is being used by Shoebat, it has a totally different meaning which is not in any way even inferred or suggested by its meaning; therefore, this is engaging in the worst kind of twisting, it is rewriting the text!

The *Complete Word Study Dictionary*, by Spiros Zodhiates, is a thick Greek dictionary that often has several definitions for a word, but it gives only one meaning for *arithmos*, NUMBER.

If John wanted to convey the meaning of a "multitude" of people, as in a group or company of people, he would have used (plethos) (4128) or "ochlos" (3793). How do I know this? Because Revelation actually contains the word "multitude" and in the Greek it is "ochlos." It appears three times 7:9; 17:15, & 19:6: *"Then I heard what sounded like a great multitude . . ."* CWD says:

> A crowd, throng, confused multitude. . . . With polloi . . . Much, great, many crowds . . . Specifically used for the common people, the rabble . . . Generally a multitude, a great number.

Therefore, if John had intended to mean "multitude" he would have used the word that actually does mean "multitude."

You may notice that the Greek, *arithmos* is the exact word from which we get our English word *arithmetic*, and *arithmetic* does not have any connection to a group or company of anything. So the correct meaning of *arithmos* is *number*, not *multitude* or *group*.

If you used this type of alternate meanings, like is described above, with any other part of the Bible, you could get anything imaginable in the text. The Bible would be a book without any predictable meaning, you could make it say anything you want.

Another thing to consider is that, since there were many Christians in the Middle East down through the centuries who were able to read and write in both Greek and Arabic, how is it that no one has seen crossed swords and *Bismillah* in the Greek text before now? Because it is not actually in the text, but is contrived to be there.

I believe the whole chapter of Rev. 13 points to Islam as I have shown in this chapter and other chapters, which are my own insights, NOT Shoebat's. The only thing of his is this nonsense I am refuting. I do not approve of Scripture twisting to show that something points to Islam. STOP the nonsense.

(5) Cannot Buy or Sell

Many people believe that there must be a literal global number in order to enforce what they believe about the mark. It says only that you must take the mark of the beast or the name of the beast, or the number of its name in order to buy or sell. This could refer to being able to conduct business. There are several Bible commentaries that agree with this point of view, such as this one:

> The text does not say that men will not be able to eat unless they have the mark . . . of the beast, but that they will not be able to carry on business without that mark. (*The Wycliffe Bible Com.* 1962) (ellipsis in the text)

Muslims are no longer among the world's most successful traders, and they blame the West. Now Western Europe and North America do most of the trading with each other and East Asia. So when the next empire comes to power, they are going to require that Christians, Jews, Hindus, and Buddhist cease doing business, thus allowing only Muslims to engage in trade in the domains which the beast controls. This was once the case in the Islamic empires.

Discrimination against Christians and Jews has been part of Islamic society since the beginning of Islam. Muhammad started *"an entire system of humiliating regulations that institutionalize*[d] *inferior status for non-Muslims in Islamic law"* (*The Politically Incorrect Guide to Islam and the Crusades*, Spencer, p. 37).

Historically, there were a host of rules that relegated non-Muslims to second-class status and were designed to make them feel inferior, demoralized, and humiliated, including heavy taxation, abduction of children, not riding horses, stepping aside for Muslims, not praying loudly, not ringing church bells, not building their houses taller than Muslims' houses, and having to wear different clothing. Some of these rules are still in place.

They frequently could not build or repair churches, or vote, or testify in a court of law, or raise their voices when singing in churches. They were even required to give three days free lodging to traveling Muslims. *"If they violate these terms, the law further stipulates that they can be killed or sold into slavery at the discretion of the Muslim leader"* (Ibid, page 51). This legal and social system of discrimination and oppression was designed to, and resulted in, a gradual conversion to Islam throughout the lands that Islam conquered. This system of *"repression, discrimination, and harassment . . . made conversion to Islam the only path to a better life"* (Ibid, page 107).

A detailed description of this social discrimination is given by Islamic expert Bat Ye'or:

> The oppressions to which those latter are exposed, even to this day, are almost incredible. In Algiers the French Government emancipated them some forty years ago, but in Tunis, Morocco, and Tripoli they only got certain liberties during the last few years. Till then they had to live in a certain quarter, and were not allowed to appear in the streets after sunset. . . . If it was a dark night they were not allowed to carry a lantern like the Moors and Turks, but a candle, which the wind extinguished every minute. They were neither allowed to ride on horseback nor on a mule,

and even to ride on a donkey was forbidden them except outside the town; they had then to dismount at the gates, and walk in the middle of the streets, so as not to be in the way of Arabs. If they had to pass the "Kasba," they had first to fall on their knees as a sign of submission, and then to walk on with lowered head; before coming to a mosque they were obliged to take the slippers off their feet, and had to pass the holy edifice without looking at it. As Tunis possesses no less than five hundred mosques, it will be seen that Jews did not wear out many shoes at that time. It was worse even in their intercourse with Musulmans; if one of these fancied himself insulted by a Jew, he stabbed him at once, and had only to pay a fine to the State, by way of punishment.

As late as 1868 seventeen Jews were murdered in Tunis without the offenders having been punished for it: often a Minister or General was in the plot, to enrich himself with the money of the murdered ones. Nor was that all. The Jews, probably to show their gratefulness for being allowed to live in the town, or to live at all, had to pay 50,000 piastres monthly to the State as a tax. (From *Protected People Under Islam*, by David G. Littman and Bat Ye'or; reprinted in *The Myth of Islamic Tolerance*, page 102.)

It is interesting to note that there were times when the Muslims were not interested in making conversions because they depended upon the tax money of non-Muslims, and actually prohibited conversions. At one point the Arabic empire put a mark on the forehead and hand of those who were _not_ Muslim, to keep them from converting because they needed the high tax income:

The kharaj, the tax on non-Muslim land, reduced the Copts to destitution: they abandoned their fields and mass conversions occurred, but they were forcibly brought back by the army and obliged to pay the taxes (694-714). To prevent the Copts from abandoning their villages, the Arab army conducted a census and branded them on the hand and brow [forehead] (705-717). No Christian could travel without a passport. Boats on the Nile that carried Christians without passports were set on fire. In 724, twenty-four thousand Copts converted to Islam to escape ruinous taxes. (A Christian Minority: The Copts in Egypt, by Bat Ye'or. Reprinted in *The Myth of Islamic Tolerance,* by R. Spencer: p. 235)

Another writer relates a horrifying account of Suleiman's tax collector, Usamah b. Zayd, in the 8th century:

> Usamah b. Zayd, used particularly barbarous means to extract money from the Christians. With hot iron bars he impressed a symbol on the body of each taxpayer. If a monk or a Christian layman was discovered without the sign, Usamah first amputated the victim's arms and then beheaded him. Many Christians converted to Islam in order to avoid punishment as well as to be freed of tribute. (Greek Christian and Other Accounts of the Muslim Conquests of the Near East, by Demetrios Constantelos, reprinted in *The Legacy of Jihad: Islamic Holy War and the Fate of Non-Muslims*, Andrew G. Bostom, page 391)

Some, but not all, of the oppressive laws were repealed in the 1800s because of pressure from European nations, which is another reason that Muslims hate Europe and America today. A missionary, named Napier Malcom, spent five years in Persia and wrote about life there in 19th century:

> Up to 1895 no Parsi [Zoroastrian] was allowed to carry an umbrella. . . . Then the houses of both the Parsis and the Jews, with the surrounding walls, had to be built so low that the top could be reached by a Mussulman with his hand extended . . . Up to about 1860 Parsis could not engage in trade. They used to hide things in their cellar rooms, and sell them secretly. They can now trade in the caravanserais or hostelries, but not in the bazaars, nor may they trade in linen drapery. Up to 1870 they were not allowed to have a school for their children. (Quoted in *The Politically Incorrect Guide to Islam and the Crusades*, by Spencer, page 162-163)

An unpublished thesis by an Egyptian relates some of the suffering which the Coptic Christians have endured:

> In short, Christians were subjected to incredible burdens by their inferiority status to Muslims in every aspect of their daily lives. They were reduced to less than slaves. In 694-714 A.D., the heavy taxes imposed on the lands of Christian Copts left them destitute. They could not possibly cultivate the land, grow crops, and pay taxes. As a result, Copts abandoned their fields and many converted to Islam. . . .

The different forms of taxes [that] were imposed on Christians were, jizya (the poll tax) and kharaj (land tax), as well as commercial and travel taxes. Apart from all of these taxes, at the ruler's will, large sums of money were extorted from Christians. If they failed to pay, he ordered <u>women and children to be taken as slaves</u>. . . . To escape the ravage of plunder, Christians were forced to pay protection money to emirs (rulers) and sheikhs (chiefs). Whenever the central government had failed to apply law and order, <u>the Muslim roving tribes took advantage of Christians</u>. To secure their lives from danger, paying protection money was part of their existence. (*The Coptic Christians of Egypt Today: Under Threat of Annihilation*, by Baheg T. Bistawros, B.D., Evangelical Theological Seminary Thesis, 1996. www.amcoptic.com/thesis.pdf)

Today Christians are discriminated against in education, employment, owning property, have their names published in the newspaper which increases social pressure by loss of employment, harassment by Muslim neighbors, and much more.

The easing of the discriminatory laws in many Muslim countries, such as no longer having to pay the heavy jizya tax, makes many modern Muslims angry and prone to attack Christians with violence. They rob them of their goods or burn down their homes and businesses.

So we see that Muslims have been punishing Christians and Jews socially and economically since the beginning of Islamic rule, and the future Islamic empire will most certainly have similar laws restricting business activity (buying and selling) by Christians and Jews, thereby forcing them to work for Muslims at low wages.

(6) Cashless Society

Most teaching on the mark of the beast today is centered around a mythical future cashless monetary system and one-world government. There is *no* worldwide conspiracy involving our government or the U.N. to bring about a cashless society ruled by the Antichrist, it's pure fiction.

The cashless system appears to be coming upon us gradually, but there will *never* be a time when ALL governments will totally convert to a cashless system. Some countries in Europe might, but that is a far cry from a global cashless society.

Consider what takes place during wars; it destroys electric lines, transformers, and power plants. Without electricity it is impossible to operate an all-electronic cash economy. Even under present conditions, there are occasional winter storms that down power lines leaving people without electricity for weeks. And in summer the heavy air conditioner usage has caused several major power outages in U.S.A. The problem is much worse in nations outside of North America and Europe; large cities may have electricity for only a limited number of hours each day. So, the lack of electricity in most nations will prevent a global cashless monetary system.

Also, the whole idea of giving everyone on Earth a mark in their forehead or right hand is preposterous and logistically impossible. It would take decades to give such a mark to more than 7 billion people. Think about how many locations would have to be set up to give out the mark; suppose there were a small number like 10,000 stations worldwide. How many years would it take to get those 10,000 stations in place? Then each station would need to give the mark to 700,000 people, which would require each station to give the mark to more than one person per minute 24 hours-a-day, 7-days-a-week, for over a year. This means that in reality it would take decades to accomplish, if ever.

We all know how inept national governments are; the U.S. government did not even get a healthcare website running correctly after several years of work in time for the start of Obamacare! Therefore, no national government could ever accomplish such a feat, certainly not a global government that will have to work with numerous languages.

When you consider that most people could not use it anyway, because the majority of the world's population doesn't even have access to a telephone or electric lights, the whole idea becomes completely absurd. Therefore, electronic cash on a global scale will NEVER happen.

Even though there will be a food shortage, it does not say that people without the mark will not be able to buy food. It just says "buy or sell," which is very general and not specific to food, so it likely refers to conducting business.

Even though the mark and number have symbolic meaning, going along with my belief that an interpretation is often multi-layered, there may actually be a literal mark which is limited to the Revived Ottoman Empire.

For example, they could require everyone to take a pledge of jihad, that they will work for the cause, even if it is only donating money, or making flags, or providing sex to the fighters. So they may require a literal mark as a sign of one's pledge of jihad, but it will not be a microchip or artificial intelligence.

There are different words in the Greek for "in" and "on," so even though the KJV says the mark will be "in" the right hand or forehead, in the Greek it says "on," which is the way it reads in most modern translations. This may seem to be a small difference, but could be significant. Being "on" the hand rather than "in" the hand rules out a microchip implant. So, if there is a literal mark, it will likely be something like Muhammad's seal or the seal of the Antichrist or Islamic Jesus.

(7) Conclusion

I want to make something clear about number of the name of the beast, 666. Even though it refers to the 2nd beast, Islam, we can expect to see it connected to the 1st beast and even to the leader, the final Antichrist. The reason is because Islam is more than a religion, it is also a ruling political system, and Islam will be the driving force behind the 1st beast. They are very much merged together.

I expect that we will yet discover more information on the number, name, and the mark of the beast as time goes by. Perhaps the name of the Mahdi will add up to 666, or the words that will be part of the mark, if there is a mark different from Muhammad's seal.

We have learned that some of the older Qurans have 6666 verses and some have 6616 verses. It is also interesting that a few of the oldest manuscripts of Rev. 13 have 616 instead of 666. The variant was even noted by the early church father, Irenaeus. This discrepancy has been examined and discussed for centuries, but I believe it is most likely 666. If it were 616 then we would expect to find things that literally add up to 616, whereas 666 is more likely to refer to multiple occurrences of the number 6, or just 666 by itself since it is far more rare and unusual than 616.

Chapter 9
The Antichrist

(1) The Mahdi

As I have said several times, and shown in this book, the beast is not a person, but earthly empires. Likewise, there have been several antichrists: Muhammad was an antichrist, as were Napoleon, Hitler, and Stalin, and there have been others. But there will surely also be a final Antichrist. The majority of the Scripture references in the Bible that speak of the Antichrist either refer to Muhammad or Allah or Islam.

In fact, the coming Islamic empire will likely have two rulers rather than one. The military and political leader will probably claim to be the Mahdi, while the religious leader, the caliph, will claim to be the returned Jesus. They will both qualify as being *Antichrist*. So in the same way that there will be two witnesses of God there could be two final Antichrists.

Most Muslims believe in the coming of the Mahdi, though belief varies even among the Shia (Shite) who hold the strongest belief in Mahdi. The Mahdi is expected to come when the world is in a state of chaos and confusion, and when Islam is oppressed. He will revive and reform Islam, and cause it *"to prevail over the various regions of the world"* (www.questionsonislam.com). He will be named Muhammad, and will be a descendant of Muhammad. The word "Mahdi" or "al-Mahdi" means *the Guided One*. He is supposed to be the next best thing to actually having Muhammad return.

The Mahdi is also supposed to find some lost Scriptures and the Ark of the Covenant which, Muslims believe, will cause many Christians and Jews to convert to Islam. Should any of those items appear, we know they will be forged, just like their book of Barnabas which is very different from the Christian book of Barnabas that was <u>not</u> included in the Bible.

Along with the Mahdi, Muslims expect the return of Jesus, who they believe was actually a Muslim. The Islamic Jesus will claim to be the real returned Jesus:

> The Hour [Day of Judgment] will not be established until the son of Mary [i.e. Jesus] descends amongst you as a just ruler, he will <u>break the cross, kill the pigs</u>, and <u>abolish the jizya tax</u>. Money will be in abundance so that nobody will accept it (as charitable gifts)." (Sahih al-Bukhari, Volume 3, Book 43, Hadith 656)

He will *"break the cross"* means to destroy Christianity. He will end the jizya tax by converting everyone to Islam. This means he will no longer allow Christians to live as subject people and pay the subjection tax, but will require them to convert or die. To kill the pigs means to kill all the Jews. So this tells us they expect to engage in <u>a massive slaughter of Christians and Jews</u>, and they will.

However, there is no way to know when the Islamic Jesus will arise; it could be at the start of the 42-month jihad or it could be a year or two later. We should not assume that it will be right away. Even if it is at the start of jihad, he may not require everyone to convert or die from the beginning, but the farther we get into WW3 the more demanding they may become, until finally requiring everyone to convert or die.

Though the Mahdi is supposed to be the caliph, the Islamic Jesus could serve as caliph while the Mahdi serves as Sultan. Muslims expect them to rule together from Jerusalem.

Even though the expectation of the Mahdi is not as strong among the Sunni as it is among the Shia, the vast majority of Muslims believe the doctrine. The chairman of the *Islamic Supreme Council of America*, Shaykh Muhammad Hisham Kabbani, said:

> The coming of the Mahdi is established doctrine for both Sunni and Shi'a Muslims, and indeed for all humanity. (Kabbani,

Shaykh Muhammad Hisham, *The Approach of Armageddon? An Islamic Perspective* (Canada, Supreme Muslim Council of America, 2003, page 228) (Quoted in *Antichrist: Islam's Awaited Messiah*, by Joel Richardson.)

A book about the Mahdi's warfare states:

. . . al-Mahdi will receive a pledge of allegiance as a caliph for Muslims. He will lead Muslims in many battles of jihad. His reign will be a caliphate that follows the guidance of the Prophet. Many battles will ensue between Muslims and the disbelievers during the Mahdi's reign. (Abdulrahman Kelani, *The Last Apocalypse, An Islamic Perspective*, Fustat, 2003, pp. 34-35) (quoted in, *Antichrist*, by Joel Richardson)

A book published in Pakistan speaks about the Mahdi said:

He will reappear on the appointed day, and then he will fight against the forces of evil [i.e. Christians and Jews], lead a world revolution and set up a new world order based on justice, right eousness and virtue [i.e. Islamic law], ultimately the righteous will take the world administration in their hands and Islam will be victorious over all the religions. (*The Awaited Savior*, by Ayatullah Baqir al-Sadr and Ayatullah Muratda Mutahhari. Islamic Seminary Publications, Karachi, page 4-5) (Quoted in, *God's War on Terror*, by Walid Shoblat, p. 93)

There have been several who claimed to be the Mahdi over the centuries. Perhaps the most well-known was Muhammad Ahmad, a Sudanese Sufi sheikh who declared himself Mahdi in June 1881. Hollywood made a movie about it in 1966 called *Khartoum* that stared Charlton Heston as the British General Gordon and Laurence Olivier as the Mahdi.

According to Zeyad Kesim, *"there are now at least seven different Mahdist sects in Iraq, each one believing that the return of the Mahdi is imminent"* (Shoebat, p. 447). The Mahdi Army in Iraq did not take its name by accident; its leader, Muqtada Al-Sadr, no doubt claims to be the Mahdi or is waiting to be proclaimed the Mahdi. They wear black, which is the color of jihad and will be the color of the Mahdi's army that will carry black flags into battle.

In addition to their two Messiahs, the Mahdi and Islamic Jesus, Muslims even have a beast and Antichrist. The problem is the Islamic Antichrist, the Dajjal, supposedly will be the Jewish Messiah and claim to be God, which is actually the real Messiah Jesus. Muslims claim their Jesus will kill the Dajjal.

(2) The Tribe of Dan?

Just as ridiculous as an Islamic Jesus, is the teaching that the real Antichrist will be a Jew from the tribe of Dan, which is what some Christians have believed since the second century. The only people alive today that identify themselves as being from Dan are a small number of black Ethiopian Jews, many or all of which are now in Israel; though some of the tribe of Dan may have gone into Europe, thus the "Danube" river that begins in Germany.

There is significant evidence in the Bible and other sources that points to great evil coming from the tribe of Dan, so the Antichrist could come from the tribe of Dan, but he will not be a Jew. How is that possible, you ask?

There is historical evidence that people from various tribes of Israel left the land of Canaan long before the Assyrian army came to carry off the ten northern tribes.

> 14 Your descendants will be like the dust of the earth, <u>and you will spread out to the west and to the east, to the north and to the south</u>. All peoples on earth will be blessed through you and your offspring. (Genesis 28:14)

Dan lived next to the Phoenicians, and it is a known fact that Danites went to sea with them and also married them. Therefore, the descendants of Dan settled in many places around the Mediterranean Sea with the Phoenicians, which has been proven by many historical researchers and does not need to be repeated here. The tribe of Dan can be traced to Africa, Cyprus, Ireland, England, Western Europe, and Greece. The book of Judges says, "*Why did Dan remain in ships?*" (5:17). The Ethreaen Sibyl calls Greeks the "*famous tribe of Danaans*" (*Visions of the End*, by Bernard McGinn, p. 123).

Josephus, the Jewish historian, acknowledged that Hebrew blood was in southern Europe. He states that Jonathan the high priest sent ambassadors to Rome and Sparta, with a letter about the kinship between Israel and the Spartans. The letter states that he is aware that the Jews are related to the Spartans, and mentions a letter that was, in years past, sent from the king of the Spartans, Areus, to the Jewish high prest, Onias, about the Spartans being related to the Jews:

> . . . although we did not need such a demonstration, because we were satisfied about it from the sacred writings yet did not we think fit first to begin the claim of this relation to you . . . although we have had many wars that have compassed us around, by reason of the covetousness of our neighbors, yet did not we determine to be troublesome either to you, or to others that were related to us . . ." (*Antiquities of the Jews*, 13:8)

The point of this is that today the Danites, perhaps those who left the land before they were carried away by Assyria as well as those who were carried away, do not know they are of the tribe of Dan. And since many people throughout North Africa and into Southern Europe eventually became Muslims, the Antichrist being from the tribe of Dan is totally realistic, even Muhammad could have some Hebrew-Danite blood in him. Also, Germany has allowed millions of Muslim refugees into the country, so the prospect of the Antichrist being of the tribe of Dan, and yet a Muslim, is very possible.

The *Testaments of the Twelve Patriarchs* says this about the tribe of Dan:

> 4 I know that in the last days ye shall depart from the Lord, And ye shall provoke Levi unto anger, And fight against Judah; But ye shall not prevail against them, For an angel of the Lord shall guide them both; For by them shall Israel stand. 5 And whensoever ye depart from the Lord, ye shall walk in all evil and work the abominations of the Gentiles, going a-whoring after women of the lawless ones, while with all wickedness the spirits 6 of wickedness work in you. . . . And there shall ye receive all the plagues of Egypt, And all the evils of the Gentiles. (From *The Apocrypha and the Apocrypha of the Pseudepigrapha of the Old Testament*, by R. H. Charles, vol. II, Oxford Press)

The above quote puts the event prophesied *"in the last days"* and says that Dan will attack Israel (Judah and Levi) but will not win the war because God is with modern Israel. It further says Dan will receive the plagues of Egypt; the Seven Bowls of Wrath in Revelation 16 are very similar to those plagues.

Irenaeus and other Early Church Fathers and writers, such as pseudo-Methodius, all believed that the Antichrist will come from the tribe of Dan. Let's examine some Biblical passages, such as Genesis 49:17:

> Dan will be a serpent by the roadside, a viper along the path, that bites the horse's heels so that its rider tumbles backward.

It seems to me this verse could describe Islamic terrorists that use roadside bombs, or snipers. In the Quran it says to "*slay the idolaters wherever you find them, and take them captives and besiege them and lie in wait for them in every ambush*" (9:5) (Shakir). Another passage in Jeremiah 8:15-17 refers to Dan:

> We hoped for peace but no good has come, for a time of healing but there was only terror. 16 The snorting of the enemy's horses is heard from Dan; at the neighing of their stallions the whole land trembles. They have come to devour the land and everything in it, the city and all who live there." 17 "See, I will send venomous snakes among you, vipers that cannot be charmed, and they will bite you," declares the LORD.

Bible commentaries about this passage will tell you that since the tribe of Dan was the northernmost tribe, and all the invaders came from the north, that they would hear of the invasion first. But notice that the tribe of Dan is again associated with snakes that bite, which is seen as an evil thing; Satan is called a serpent.

Another point made about Dan being connected to the Antichrist is that the tribe of Dan is missing from the list of tribes in Revelation 7, in the counting of the 144,000. But this is not as significant as the above verses.

The other verses some people use to connect Dan to the Antichrist do not even have a hint of anything negative about Dan, but actually have positive statements, such as craftsmen from Dan working to make the items inside the Tabernacle of Moses. This supposedly refers to Freemasons who supposedly will have a connection to a European Antichrist and Revived Roman Empire, which is not the case.

So if the Antichrist has Hebrew blood in him from the tribe of Dan, it does not make him a Jew. Many people of the world have Hebrew blood, including Muslims, but don't know it. According to the Hadiths, Muhammad made war against several Jewish tribes and took three of the women to be his sex slaves: Juwairiya, Safiyah, and Rayhanah. The other women were distributed among his soldiers. And there must have been some babies born from those rapes (www.faithfreedom.org/challenge/rapist.htm).

And over the centuries, some Jews even converted under pressure, so the statement by Jesus that another will come in his own name and they will accept him likely does <u>not</u> refer to all the Jews, but only a small number of the Jews who would end up becoming Muslims.

Seriously, do you really believe that the Muslims of the world are going to be deceived and follow after a Jewish world leader who claims to be God, and worship him? Total lunacy. Or vice versa? This is simply not the case. The Muslims are not going to follow any Jewish leader, EVER! Nor will they follow any European leader, unless he is a Muslim, and they are not going to allow the Jews to rebuild their Temple (see BK1).

Muslims are brainwashed from birth to hate the Jews and want them all dead. But will there be a Jewish Temple next to the Dome of the Rock? The Muslims say, *"We knock on the gates of heaven with the skulls of Jews"* (Shoebat, *God's War on Terror*, page 163). TAKE YOUR BLINDERS OFF! There will never be a more Jew-hating, blood-loving, Christ-hating people on Earth than the Muslims! Therefore, the Antichrist will be a Muslim, not a Jew!

(3) The Assyrian

There are several passages in the Old Testament prophecies that refer to the Antichrist as *the Assyrian*; therefore, many Bible teachers believe that he will come from the region of Assyria, which was northern Iraq and Iran, and southern Turkey. There are still many people living there today that refer to themselves as Assyrians, but most, if not all, are Christians.

It is likely that the term *"the Assyrian"* is being used because it refers to the original Assyrian, Sennacherib, as a type of the future Antichrist, not where he will originate, though it is possible he will have a residence there. Sennacherib invaded Israel and killed many Israelites and carried many off into slavery. Likewise, the future Antichrist will do the same.

Let's examine some of the passages that reference *the Assyrian*. Isaiah 14 supposedly refers to the king of Babylon, but also to Satan, but it also refers to the Antichrist. History knows of no king of Babylon that was left unburied, as the man in Isaiah 14 will be; therefore, that part does not refer to any historical king of Babylon:

> 3 On the day the LORD gives you relief from suffering and turmoil and cruel bondage, 4 you will take up this taunt against the king of Babylon: How the oppressor has come to an end! How his fury has ended!

The first question to be answered is, does this chapter refer to ancient Babylon, or Mystery Babylon? Or perhaps some other? An examination of the chapter reveals no points of reference that point to modern America, as is the case in Jeremiah 50 and 51. This chapter appears to reference an individual only, and his death. Here is the Literal translation of verse 4:

> . . . How the exacter, the gold gatherer, has ceased.

The English translation of the LXX, says:

> How has the extortioner ceased, and the taskmaster ceased!

In the Hebrew, it refers to heavy taxes extracted from the population. Most translations say "oppressor." Barne's Notes says, *"The word 'oppressor' (מַדְהֵבָה) denotes, properly, the 'exactor of tribute'. . ."* Who has been noted in this book for high taxation on Christians and Jews? All Islamic empires, so I believe this passage refers to the future Antichrist, as the land of Babylon is today Islamic. Isaiah 14 continues:

5 The LORD has broken the rod of the wicked, the scepter of the rulers, 6 which in anger struck down peoples with unceasing blows, and in fury subdued nations with relentless aggression. 7 All the lands are at rest and at peace; they break into singing. 8 Even the pine trees and the cedars of Lebanon exult over you and say, "Now that you have been laid low, no woodsman comes to cut us down."

Notice, that in verse 8 the cedars of Lebanon rejoice that they no longer are killed or oppressed. Lebanon is located in the Middle East, just north of Israel, south of Syria. Isaiah 14 continues:

9 The grave below is all astir to meet you at your coming; it rouses the spirits of the departed to greet you— all those who were leaders in the world; it makes them rise from their thrones— all those who were kings over the nations.

10 They will all respond, they will say to you, "You also have become weak, as we are; you have become like us."

11 All your pomp has been brought down to the grave, along with the noise of your harps; maggots are spread out beneath you and worms cover you.

Again this appears to refer to an individual. In the next section of verses, there is a shift from the king of Babylon, to Lucifer himself, but the statements also fit an individual man:

12 How you have fallen from heaven, O morning star, son of the dawn! You have been cast down to the earth, you who once laid low the nations! 13 You said in your heart, "I will ascend to heaven; I will raise my throne above the stars of God; I will sit enthroned on the mount of assembly, on the utmost heights of the sacred mountain. 14 I will ascend above the tops of the clouds; I will make myself like the Most High."

15 But you are brought down to the grave, to the depths of the pit. 16 Those who see you stare at you, they ponder your fate: "Is this the man who shook the earth and made kingdoms tremble, 17 the man who made the world a desert, who overthrew its cities and would not let his captives go home?" 18 All the kings of the nations lie in state, each in his own tomb.

19 But you are cast out of your tomb like a rejected branch; you are covered with the slain, with those pierced by the sword,

those who descend to the stones of the pit. Like a corpse trampled underfoot, 20 <u>you will not join them in burial</u>, for you have destroyed your land and killed your people. The offspring of the wicked will never be mentioned again. . . .

25 <u>I will crush the Assyrian in my land</u>; on my mountains I will trample him down. . . ." (Is. 14:12-20, 25)

The most astonishing thing about this information is that some Bible commentaries say it does not refer to Satan, but to the king of Babylon, as if the king of Babylon was cast down from heaven. I believe most of the passage refers to Satan and Mohammad, the original Antichrist.

It is surprising that no one has seen that it describes Muhammad. *"You said in your heart, "I will ascend to heaven; I will raise my throne above the stars of God."* This sounds boastful, and proud, which fits Muhammad and Muslims in general, as we have already seen. It says, basically, he will become greater than Jesus and the righteous saints of God, which Muhammad tried to do with his invented religion. But even more to the point, Muhammad actually claimed to have ascended to heaven where he was given a ride on a *Buraq*, a mythical creature with the body of a horse and the head of a man, which supposedly took him to the Temple Mount in Jerusalem, then back to Arabia. (I don't know if he invented this creature or if it was already believed to exist prior to Muhammad's time.) Because of this tale, the Dome of the Rock was built that covers a stone that is supposed to contain the footprint of Muhammad. It is not a mosque, but a shrine to the stone and Muhammad. (The Temple Mount also contains the Al-Aqsa Mosque.)

It says, *"I will sit enthroned on the mount of assembly, on the utmost heights of the sacred mountain"* (v.13). Walid Shoebat, in *God's War on Terror*, sees the Antichrist in this verse sitting in the rebuilt Jewish Temple, but it fits Muhammad because he lifted himself up higher than all other prophets, and even the Son of God. And the Dome of the Rock is a shine to Muhammad built on the Holy Mount of God, Mount Moriah.

The night journey of Muhammad.

http://en.wikipedia.org/wiki/Buraq

The part about being left unburied and trampled upon seems to refer to the final Antichrist who will be a follower of, and type of, Muhammad. People frequently speak of someone being a forerunner of the Antichrist, but Muhammad was the original Antichrist, and the Mahdi and Islamic Jesus will be the final Antichrists. So this passage likely refers to one of them.

Now let's look at a passage that is generally overlooked because Bible commentators believe it only speaks about Egypt. But what they cannot figure out is why Ezekiel 31 mentions "*the Assyrian*" while talking about Egypt. It is because part of the description also applies to the future Antichrist. But what is even more confounding is that it says the Assyrian will be from Lebanon! Does this mean one of the two final Antichrists will actually be from Lebanon? In the Bible Jesus was said to be both from Bethlehem and Egypt, because he was born in Bethlehem but taken to Egypt as a child. Therefore, one of the Antichrists could grow up in Lebanon, or have ancestry from Lebanon. But the passage also applies to Satan because no Egyptian or Assyrian was in the Garden of Eden:

> Behold, the Assyrian was a cedar in Lebanon with fair branches, and with a shadowing shroud, and of an high stature; and his top was among the thick boughs. . . . 9 I have made him fair by the multitude of his branches: so that all the trees of Eden, that were in the garden of God, envied him. (Ezek. 31:3, 9) (KJV)

Many modern translations do not have the word, "the" before "Assyrian" but it clearly refers to one person which is often referred to as, "him" or "he." Therefore, "the" should be included, which is why some translations include it. There are other passages that also refer to *"the Assyrian"* but the newer translations are less likely to have "the" in the text.

(4) Satan or Muhammad?

As we have seen in the above sections, some passages appear to speak of Satan but also the final Antichrist, but sometimes the verses seem to speak about Muhammad or even Allah, as seen in Daniel 11. Ezekiel 28 is another such passage. I urge you to read this whole passage. I could underline almost every line, but that would defeat the purpose of underlining:

> The word of the LORD came to me: 2 "Son of man, say to the ruler of Tyre, 'This is what the Sovereign LORD says: 'In the pride of your heart you say, "I am a god; I sit on the throne of a god in the heart of the seas." But you are a man and not a god, though you think you are as wise as a god. 3 Are you wiser than Daniel? Is no secret hidden from you? 4 By your wisdom and understanding you have gained wealth for yourself and amassed gold and silver in your treasuries. 5 By your great skill in trading you have increased your wealth, and because of your wealth your heart has grown proud. 6 "'Therefore this is what the Sovereign LORD says: "'Because you think you are wise, as wise as a god, 7 I am going to bring foreigners against you, . . . 8 They will bring you down to the pit, and you will die a violent death in the heart of the seas. 9 Will you then say, "I am a god," in the presence of those who kill you? You will be but a man, not a god, in the hands of those who slay you. 10 You will die the death of the uncircumcised at the hands of foreigners. I have

spoken, declares the Sovereign LORD.'"

11 The word of the LORD came to me: 12"Son of man, take up a lament <u>concerning the king of Tyre</u> and say to him: 'This is what the Sovereign LORD says: "'You were the <u>model of perfection, full of wisdom and perfect in beauty</u>. 13 You were in <u>Eden, the garden of God</u>; every precious stone adorned you: ruby, topaz and emerald, chrysolite, onyx and jasper, sapphire, turquoise and beryl. Your settings and mountings were made of gold; on the day you were created they were prepared. 14 You were anointed as a guardian cherub, for so I ordained you. <u>You were on the holy mount of God; you walked among the fiery stones</u>. 15 You were blameless in your ways from the day you were created till wickedness was found in you. 16 <u>Through your widespread trade you were filled with violence, and you sinned</u>. So I drove you in disgrace from the mount of God, and I expelled you, O guardian cherub, from among the fiery stones. 17 <u>Your heart became proud</u> on account of your beauty, and you corrupted your wisdom because of your splendor. So <u>I threw you to the earth</u>; I made a spectacle of you before kings. 18 By your many sins and <u>dishonest trade</u> you have desecrated your sanctuaries. So I made a <u>fire come out from you, and it consumed you, and I reduced you to ashes on the ground</u> in the sight of all who were watching. 19 All the nations who knew you are appalled at you; you have come to a horrible end and will be no more.'"

Part of the above passage clearly refers to Satan, but did he ever work as a trader here on Earth? Here are some interesting parallels to Muhammad in the above passages:

Verses 4-5, 16:

> * Muhammad was a successful, wealthy trader, who became a violent warrior.

Verses 6, 12:

> * Muhammad was lifted up in pride, claiming great revelations and knowledge. Muslims claim that Muhammad was the perfect human, (al-Insān al-Kāmil).

The wording of verse 12 is even more shocking in other translations:

> * You were the <u>seal of perfection</u>, full of wisdom and perfect in beauty. (NKJV)

* You had the seal of perfection, full of wisdom and beauty. (NASB)

We have already learned that Muhammad was supposed to be *"the seal of the prophets,"* and this passage refers to someone who is called *"the seal of perfection."* Muhammad also was supposedly the perfect man. In verse 18 it describes a person who is consumed by fire and reduced to ashes, which does not refer to Satan or Muhammad but to the final Antichrist(s).

Also, the city of Tyre was located in Phoenicia, which is modern-day Lebanon, so a ruler of Tyre today is a Muslim, but there are still a good number of Christians there.

Walid Shoebat quotes Islamic sources that show the extent to which Muhammad is exalted and seen as perfect:

> "Allah . . . describes the personality of Muhammad (PBUH) in these words: 'And you stand on an exalted standard of character' (Holy Quran 68: v. 4). Thus in the words of Allah, the standard of his character and personality is far above that of any other creation. He possessed the best and noblest qualities of the perfect man and was like a jewel illuminating the dark environment with his radiant personality, ideal example, and glorious message." Islam requires all Muslims to believe that Mohammed is literally the best of all God's creation. . . . In order to support this idea, Muslims often point out that throughout the Quran, Allah has actually shared many of his names with Mohammed. This is viewed as a clear proof that from among all of the created order, Mohammed holds a uniquely exalted status unparalleled by anything or anyone else. He is given the title Al-Maqam-Mahmud (The Glorious). (Shoebat, *God's War on Terror*, p. 142-143)

You can see that Muslims have exalted Muhammad to be only a little lower than Allah himself, and Allah and Muhammad share the same name. Therefore, when Muhammad gave those "revelations" he was exalting himself to near the status of a god, as we just read in Ezekiel 28, thinking himself to be brilliant.

(5) Daniel 8

In Daniel 8 we have a vision in which Daniel sees a ram that is attacked and killed by a more powerful goat. The latter one was Greece that conquered the Media-Persian Empire. The vision is about Alexander the Great, followed by Antiochus Epiphanies who set up the first Abomination of Desolation, but it is also about the end times and the final Antichrist. So it is partly a double-fulfillment prophecy, because it tells us clearly that it jumps to the end time and describes what can only be Islamic terrorists and the final Antichrist:

> 19 He said: "I am going to tell you what will happen later in the time of wrath, because the vision concerns the appointed time of the end. . . .
>
> 23 "In the latter part of their reign [the two goats], when rebels have become completely wicked, a stern-faced king, a master of intrigue, will arise.
>
> 24 He will become very strong, but not by his own power. He will cause astounding devastation and will succeed in whatever he does. He will destroy the mighty men and the holy people.
>
> 25 He will cause deceit to prosper, and he will consider himself superior. When they feel secure, he will destroy many and take his stand against the Prince of princes. Yet he will be destroyed, but not by human power. (Dan. 8)

The passage seems to speak about the final Antichrist, but could easily refer to Muhammad and Islam, because the description certainly does fit both. Mohammed slaughtered many Jews and Christians, and exalted himself. He also became strong by the power of Satan. And he took a stand against Jesus being the Son of God, as already quoted from the Quran.

It says that he will be destroyed, but not by human power. Muhammad died while having severe pain in his head. Muslims claim it was the result of being poisoned by a Jewish woman. The final Antichrist(s) could be killed by nuclear weapons, but more likely by as asteroid impacts. If not, then they will most certainly die in another fire that comes upon the world at the return of Christ (BK4). So, again, Dan. 8 could refer to Muhammad and Islam, or to the final Antichrist(s) who will be killed by God.

The phrase, *"When they feel secure, he will destroy many"* is one of the reasons people think that the Antichrist will come to power by bringing world peace. But it is more likely that he will sign a peace agreement just before World War 3 breaks out, or just before he invades some nearby nations. It does NOT require that he comes to power by bringing world peace; he is likely already in power and acting regionally. Hitler also made peace agreements with his neighbors just before he invaded them, which started WW2.

Even though the passage describes Muhammad, it clearly must also include the final Antichrist(s) because it plainly refers to the very end that includes the Wrath of God upon the world. The GW translation of verse 19 says:

> He said, "I will tell you what will happen in the last days, the time of God's anger, because the end time has been determined. . . .

The phrase, *"rebels have become completely wicked,"* no doubt refers to terrorism. We saw throughout this book, examples of Islamic terrorism. Here are some of Muhammad's other statements about violence:

> Allah's Apostle said, "I have been made victorious with terror (cast in the hearts of the enemy) . . ." (Bukhari: Volume 52, Book 4, Hadith 220)

> I will cast terror into the hearts of those who disbelieve. Therefore strike off their heads and strike off every fingertip of them. (Quran 8:12)

> O you who believe! fight those of the unbelievers who are near to you and let them find in you hardness. (Quran 9:123)

> If the hypocrites, and those in whose hearts is a disease, and the alarmists in the city do not cease, We verily shall urge thee on against them, then they . . . will be seized wherever found and slain with a (fierce) slaughter. (Quran 33:60-62)

> Allah 's Apostle said, "I have been ordered to fight with the people till they say, 'None has the right to be worshipped but Allah,'. . ." (Book 56, Hadith 158; Narrated by Abu Huraira. http://sunnah.com/bukhari/56)

You may think that this is a short chapter on the Antichrist, because whole books have been written about him, but those books are full of great speculation. There is very little in the Bible that is actually about an individual known as Antichrist. Most of this book is about the final beast and false prophet, which have in the past been seen as the Antichrist and his religion, but we now know they are a final empire and the religion of that empire. Since this book was first written I have learned the identity of one of the Antichrists and wrote 120 page book presenting the evidence to support his identity, which is *The Final Antichrist Barack Obama*. It speaks about his history and evidence that he is a Muslim and what he has done against Christianity and prophecies about him being the Antichrist and what he will do in the near future.

Chapter 10
Historical Views

(1) The Early Christians and Jews

There were no newspapers to document the Islamic invasion of the Eastern Roman Empire, but a few documents have survived which tell us that <u>the Christians believed that Islam and Muhammad were the beasts of Revelation 13</u>.

One of the earliest references to the Islamic invasions is found in *The Panegyric of the Three Holy Children of Babylon*; the writer is unknown, but describes the invaders as *"oppressors who follow after prostitution and massacre."* (Prof. Dr. Harald Suermann, of the Institute of Oriental and Asian Studies, Bonn University, *Copts and the Islam of the Seventh Century.* Published in, *Christian-Muslim Relations; A Bibliographical History*, Volume 5; David Thomas, p. 114.)

According to *History of the Christian Church*, by Philip Schaff, the Christians of that era and beyond viewed Muhammad as the Antichrist:

> The mediaeval writers, both Greek and Latin, represent Mohammed as an impostor and arch-heretic, who wove his false religion chiefly from Jewish (Talmudic) fables and Christian heresies. They find him foretold in <u>the Little Horn of Daniel</u>, and <u>the False Prophet of the Apocalypse</u>. . . . Even the mild and scholarly Melanchthon identifies Mohammed with the Little Horn of Daniel, or rather with the Gog and Magog of the Apocalypse. (chapter 3)

John, Bishop of Nikiu, was probably born about the time of the Islamic invasion of Egypt. He was a Coptic bishop and rector of the bishops of Upper Egypt. He wrote a history that says:

> And when those Moslem, accompanied by the Egyptians who had apostatized from the Christian faith and embraced the faith of the beast, had come up, the Moslem took as a booty all the possessions of the Christians who had fled, and they designated the servants of Christ enemies of God. . . . (*Chronicle*, Chapter CXIV (114))

In another chapter he said:

> And now many of the Egyptians who had been false Christians denied the holy orthodox faith and life-giving baptism, and embraced the religion of the Moslem, the enemies of God, and accepted the detestable doctrine of the beast, this is, Mohammed, and they erred together with those idolaters, and took arms in their hands and fought against the Christians. And one of them, named John, the Chalcedonian of the Convent of Sinai, embraced the faith of Islam, and quitting his monk's habit he took up the sword, and persecuted the Christians who were faithful to our Lord Jesus Christ. (Chapter CXXI (121), 1916 translation by R. H. Charles, at www.tertul lian.org.)

The Bishop twice refers to Muhammad as the beast, which is clear enough, and he gave evidence of violent persecution of Christians. Sophronius, Patriarch of Jerusalem, was an eyewitness to the invasions; he wrote:

> That is why the vengeful and God-hating Saracens, the abomination of desolation clearly foretold to us by the prophets, overrun the places which are not allowed to them, plunder cities, devastate fields, burn down villages, set on fire the holy churches, overturn the sacred monasteries, oppose the Byzantine armies arrayed against them, and in fighting raise up the trophies (of war) and add victory to victory.

> Moreover, they are raised up more and more against us and increase their blasphemy of Christ and the church, and utter wicked blasphemies against God. Those God-fighters boast of prevailing over all, assiduously and unrestrainedly imitating their leader, who is the devil, and emulating his vanity because of which he has been expelled from heaven and been assigned to the gloomy shades. Yet these vile ones would not have accomplished this nor seized such a degree of power as to do and utter

lawlessly all these things, unless we had first insulted the gift (of baptism) and first defiled the purification, and in this way grieved Christ, the giver of gifts, and prompted him to be angry with us, good though he is and though he takes no pleasure in evil, being the fount of kindness and not wishing to behold the ruin and destruction of men. We are ourselves, in truth, responsible for all these things and no word will be found for our defense. What word or place will be given us for our defense when we have taken all these gifts from him, befouled them and defiled everything with our vile actions? (sermon on *Holy Baptism.* Quoted in *Seeing Islam as Others Saw It: A Survey and Evaluation of Christian, Jewish and Zoroastrian Writings on Early Islam,* by Robert G. Hoyland, 1997. pp. 72-73)

Notice that he stated the cause of the invasions were the many sins of the Christians. Maximus the Confessor (580-662) in Alexandria, Egypt, wrote a letter (634-640) to Peter the Illustrious which included his thoughts on the Islamic invasions:

For what could be more dire than the present evils now encompassing the civilized world? . . . To see a barbarous nation of the desert overrunning another land as if it were their own! To see our civilization [*politeia*] laid waste by wild and untamed beasts who have merely the shape of a human form! . . . delight in human blood . . . (*Medieval Christian Perceptions of Islam,* John Victor Tolan, editor. Routledge, New York, 1996, p. 14-15)

He goes on to express his belief that the causes of the Arabs' success are the sins of the Christians, *"For we have not conducted ourselves in a manner worthy of the Gospel of Christ"* (Ibid). The Christians were having big disputes about doctrine in those days and persecuting those Christians who believed in doctrines that happen to be out of favor. Maximus later had his tongue cut out by Christians so he could not spread his doctrinal views and his hand cut off so he could no longer write his beliefs, and died shortly thereafter. No wonder God allowed the Muslims to make war against the Christians!

A monk named Anastasius made references to the Islamic invasions, about A.D. 660:

Note well that <u>the demons name the Saracens as their compan-</u>

ions. And it is with reason. The latter are perhaps even worse than the demons. Indeed, the demons are frequently much afraid of the mysteries of Christ, I mean his holy body. . . , the cross, the saints, the relics, the holy oils and many other things. But these demons of flesh trample all that is under their feet, mock it, set fire to it, destroy it ... (*Encouraging and supportive tales of the most humble monk Anastasius, which occurred in various places in our times*. In, *Seeing Islam*, by R. Hoyland, page 100-101)

Anastasius also said:

When Heraclius died, Martin was exiled by Heraclius' grandson and immediately the desert dweller Amalek rose up to strike us, Christ's people. That was the first terrible and fatal defeat of the Roman army. I am speaking of the bloodshed at Gabitha, Yarmuk and Dathemon, after which occurred the capture and burning of the cities of Palestine, even Caesarea and Jerusalem. Then there was the destruction of Egypt, followed by the enslavement and fatal devastations of the Mediterranean lands and islands and of all the Roman empire. But the rulers and masters of the Romans did not manage to perceive these things. Rather they summoned the most eminent men in the Roman church, and had their tongues and hands excised. And what then? The retribution upon us from God for these things was the almost complete loss of the Roman army and navy at Phoenix, and the progressive desolation of all the Christian people and places. . . . (Ibid, page 102-103)

A Jew named Justus heard about the Arab invasions and wrote that some of the Jews, who were being persecuted by the Romans, were wondering or hoping that Muhammad was Elijah, and that Messiah would follow:

When the candidatus [a Roman official] was killed by the Saracens, I was at Caesarea and I set off by boat to Sykamina. People were saying "the candidatus has been killed," and we Jews were overjoyed. And they were saying that the prophet had appeared, coming with the Saracens, and that he was proclaiming the advent of the anointed one, the Christ who was to come. I, having arrived at Sykamina, stopped by a certain old man well-versed in the scriptures, and I said to him: "What can you tell me about the prophet who has appeared with the Saracens?" He replied, groaning deeply: "He is false, for the prophets do not come armed with a sword. Truly they are works of anarchy being committed today and I fear that the first Christ to come, whom the Christians worship, was the one sent by God and we instead are preparing to receive the Antichrist. Indeed, Isaiah said that the Jews would retain a perverted and hardened heart until all the earth should be devastated. But you go, master Abraham, and find out about the prophet who has appeared." So I, Abraham, inquired and heard from those who had met him that there was no truth to be found in the so-called prophet, only the shedding of men's blood. He says also that he has the keys of paradise, which is incredible. (Doctrina Jacobi V.16, 209) (*Seeing Islam as Others Saw It*, by R. G. Hoyland, page 57)

Based on the many sources in *Seeing Islam as Others Saw It*, Robert G. Hoyland gives us a brief summary of events in the first 100 years of Islam:

> Destruction of crosses, construction on the site of the Temple, removal of the cross from the coinage, conversion of the church of John the Baptist in Damascus into a mosque, and outbreaks of apostasy . . . The order of Yazid II in 721 that "the crosses should be broken in every place and that the pictures which were in the church should be removed" . . . (page 104)

The following was written on a page of a Bible of that time:

> In January {the people of} Hims took the word for their lives and many villages were ravaged by the killing of {the followers of} Muhammad (*Muhmd*) and many people were slain and {taken} prisoner from Galilee as far as Beth. . . .
>
> On the tenth {of August} the Romans fled from the vicinity of Damascus {and there were killed} many {people}, some ten thousand. . . . (Ibid, page 117) (The brackets {}() are in Hoyland.)

The "word" they took for their lives refers to the Bible. They died as Christian martyrs and did not deny Christ by converting to Islam.

A book was written in Spain in the late 600s and circulated throughout Europe; it pointed to Muhammad as the Antichrist. According to the Spanish calendar that was ahead of other calendars, Muhammad died in the year 666, so they said Muhammad was the Antichrist, which was an understandable assumption.

Moses Maimonides (1135-1204) was a famous Jewish Scholar who was persecuted in Islamic Spain; he said:

> The nation of Ishmael persecutes us severely and devises ways to harm us and to debase us. None has been able to reduce us as they have. We have done as our sages instructed us, bearing the lies and absurdities of Ishmael. We listen but remain silent. In spite of all this, we are not spared from the ferocity of their wickedness and their outbursts at any time. On the contrary, the more we suffer and choose to conciliate them, the more they choose to act belligerently toward us. (Bill Warner, Director, *Center for the Study of Political Islam*, www.political-islam. com/blog/ partners-in-crime/ April 6, 2012)

Notice the last line above; many times in history it is noted that when you act conciliatory toward Muslims they will attack you all the more, and so the only appropriate response is to fight them.

(2) What the Later Catholics and Protestants Believed

According to the *Encyclopedia of Religion and Ethics* (1951), Pope Innocent III in 1215, *"denounced the Saracenes as Antichrist and Muhammad as the false prophet"* (Royston Pyke, p. 20).

The next quote not only tells us what Christians like Gregory Palamus of Thessalonica (1354) thought of the Muslims, but it also reveals the character and nature of Islam:

> For these impious people, hated by God and infamous, boast of having got the better of the Romans by their love of God. . . . they live by the bow, the sword and debauchery, finding pleasure in taking slaves, devoting themselves to murder, pillage, spoil . . . and not only do they commit these crimes, but even — what an aberration — they believe that God approves of them. This is what I think of them, now that I know precisely about their way of life. (Quoted in Spencer, *The Politically Incorrect Guide to Islam and the Crusades*, page 41)

An authoritative book on the destruction of Constantinople by the Turks states that while the Muslim armies were camped outside the city walls in 1453, the Christians remembered the prophecies that spoke about the destruction of the empire:

> There were one or two slight earthquakes and some torrential rains, all of them interpreted as evil omens, while men and women reminded themselves of all the <u>prophecies that foretold the end of the Empire and the coming of Anti-Christ</u>. (*The Fall of Constantinople 1453*, by Steven Runciman, 1965, page 79)

It seems as though he said the prophecies said the Eastern Roman Empire would end followed by the coming of Antichrist, but he was actually saying that they were the same event; the destruction of the empire was done by the followers of Antichrist.

When the last Emperor of the Roman Empire knew that he was about to be defeated by the Muslims, he gave a final speech to his court before the Muslims breeched the walls of the city:

> He spoke of the perfidy of the infidel Sultan who had provoked the war in order to destroy the True Faith and to put his <u>false prophet in the seat of Christ</u>. (Ibid, page 130)

As time passed, Protestantism rose up, and even the Protestant reformers such as Martin Luther saw Muhammad as the Antichrist in the east and the pope as the Antichrist in the west. This dual Antichrist view remained popular into the 19th century, and some people still believe it this way.

In 1713 John Floyer published the first English translation of the *Sibylline Oracles* and included a comparison of the oracles with Daniel and Revelation. Floyer was physician to the Queen and invented the second hand on watches in order to count a patient's pulse; he believed that Muhammad was the Antichrist:

> The history of Mahomet [Muhammad] shows that he is that Antichrist described by Irenaeus . . . (*The Sibylline Oracles,* Floyer, page 227)

> [A] comet appeared at the time of his death resembling a sword, pointing from south to north; this continued thirty days, and appeared at mid-day, and it preceded or portended the rise of the Arabian Monarchy. (Ibid, p. 231)

> The Mahometans are the Antichrist in the east, who by their op-

pressions forced Christians to forsake Christ to follow Mahomet's doctrine. . . . (Ibid, page 247)

Though Floyer was a Protestant, he makes a strong argument for Muhammad being the Antichrist instead of the pope:

That the pope is not Antichrist, these are my arguments:

1. He [the pope] never denied the Father and the Son, which is St. John's mark of the great Antichrist.

2. It is nowhere said that Antichrist must be a Christian, but as his name implies, the adversary to that religion. He may be said to sit in the Temple who turned it into a mosque, and built one on the ruins of Solomon's Temple, as Omar did. . . .

6. In the Turkish prayers they use the following epithet of God; Rabol Maizza, the Lord of Powers or Fortitudes, which is the same with Eloah Mauzzi, Dan. 11:31, which is the title of God omnipotent, and the words of the prayer are these: *Be that far from you, O Lord, O Lord of Powers; which they* (Christians) *attribute to you,* (that you are a father, and has a wife and son). This is a public profession against the Father and Son, and the most evident character of Antichrist, and not of the pope. (Floyer, p. 324-326)

Here is what John Wesley said about Islam later in the 18th century:

Ever since the religion of Islam appeared in the world, the espousers of it . . . have been as wolves and tigers to all other nations, rending and tearing all that fell into their merciless paws, and grinding them with their iron teeth; that numberless cities are raised from the foundation, and only their name remaining; that many countries, which were once as the garden of God, are now a desolate wilderness; and that so many once numerous and powerful nations are vanished from the earth! Such was, and is at this day, the rage, the fury, the revenge, of these destroyers of human kind. (*The Doctrine of Original Sin, Works* (1841). Quoted in *The Politically Incorrect Guide to Islam And the Crusades*, by R. Spencer, p. 188.)

Jonathan Edwards wrote that the pope, paganism, and Islam will all be in an alliance against true Christianity:

It seems as though in this last great opposition which shall be made against the church to defend the kingdom of Satan, all the forces of Antichrist, and Mahometanism, and Heathenism, will be united; all the forces of Satan's visible kingdom through the whole world of mankind. . . . there shall be a spirit of Popery, and the spirit of Mahometanism, and the spirit of Heathenism all united. (*The Works of President Edwards, in Four Volumes.* Vol. 1, 1852, page 484.)

Sir Winston Churchill certainly did not speak conciliatory about Islam and Muslims, like our spineless leaders today; he spoke boldly:

How dreadful are the curses which Mohammedanism lays on its votaries! Besides the fanatical frenzy, which is as dangerous in a man as hydrophobia in a dog, there is this fearful fatalistic apathy. The effects are apparent in many countries. Improvident habits, slovenly systems of agriculture, sluggish methods of commerce and insecurity of property exist wherever the followers of the Prophet rule or live . . . The fact that in Mohammedan law every woman must belong to some man as his absolute property, either as a child, a wife, or a concubine, must delay the final extinction of slavery until the faith of Islam has ceased to be a great power among men. Individual Moslems may show splendid qualities . . . but the influence of the religion paralyzes the social development of those who follow it. No stronger retrograde force exists in the world. Far from being moribund, Mohammedanism is a militant and proselytizing faith. It has already spread throughout Central Africa . . . and were it not that Christianity is sheltered in the strong arms of science, the science against which it had vainly struggled, the civilisation of modern Europe might fall, as fell the civilisation of ancient Rome. (Winston Churchill, *The River War*, Vol. II, pp. 248-50, London; Longman, Green & Co., 1899)

G.K. Chesterton (1874-1936) wrote in 1917:

The great creed born in the desert creates a kind of ecstasy of the very emptiness of its own land, and even, one may say, out of the emptiness of its own theology. . . . A void is made in the heart of Islam which has to be filled up again and again by a mere <u>repetition of the revolution that founded it</u>. There are no sacraments; <u>the only thing that can happen is a sort of apoca-lypse</u>, as unique as the end of the world . . . (Chesterton, *Lord Kitchener*, p. 8)

Hilaire Belloc (1870-1953) was a French writer, historian, political activist, and also a bold Catholic. In 1938 he wrote:

> But I ask the question in the sense "Will not perhaps the temporal power of Islam return and with it the menace of an armed Mohammedan world, which will shake off the domination of Europeans -- still nominally Christian -- and reappear as the prime enemy of our civilization?" The future always comes as a surprise, but political wisdom consists in attempting at least some partial judgment of what that surprise may be. And for my part I cannot but believe that a main unexpected thing of the future is the return of Islam. (*The Great Heresies*, p. 63.)

Bishop Fulton J Sheen said in a book published in 1950:

> Today, the hatred of the Moslem countries against the West is becoming hatred against Christianity itself. Although the statesmen have not yet taken it into account, there is still grave danger that the temporal power of Islam may return and, with it, the menace that it may shake off a West which has ceased to be Christian, and affirm itself [Islam] as a great anti-Christian world Power. (*The World's First Love*, 1996, p. 201)

Apparently the Bishop was not fully aware of Islamic history, because Muslims have always followed Muhammad's command to be "*ruthless to the unbelievers*" (Quran 48:29). All this evidence shows that Osama Bin Laden was not triggered by the presence of the U.S.A. in the Middle East. The Muslims have hated the West and desired to bring destruction upon us since the beginning of Islam.

Chapter 11
Final Words

There is additional information pointing to Islam in BK1, for example: the fourth horseman of the Apocalypse is the spread of Islam, because the horse is green, not pale as in the English translations. The little horn of Daniel is also covered in BK1, and much more.

I could say a lot more about Islam in America but there are already several books and websites that cover that subject in great detail. The main purpose of this book is to show the history of Turkey and Islam, and how they are planning another empire, and how they will be the final head of the beast and false prophet of Revelation 13.

You cannot depend on the liberal media to tell you the truth about Islam. It is like they are spiritually blind. They continue to report good things about local Muslims even when it has been proven that they actually teach violence, and that Europe and America must be destroyed. Those who do speak the truth are called intolerant racists. This is happening in Europe, Canada, and America. (www.peaceandtolerance.org)

We thought our enemy, the Soviet Communists, were defeated, but the Communists are still working behind the scenes in Russia, and even here in America; they merely changed their names to Progressive Democrats. So the Communist threat here in America is as great as ever because there are actually more Progressives here than ever were old Communists. And now they are colluding with Muslims.

You know the old saying, *"The enemy of my enemy is my*

friend," well, Communists and Muslims are working together to destroy America, it is being called the Red-Green alliance. Their armies will fight together against America in World War 3.

At this moment Muslim armies are waging war against Christians in Sudan and Nigeria, and an unofficial war is being waged against Christians in Iraq, Libya, Egypt, and especially Syria. Pastor Moti Cohen wrote a chilling report on what is happening in Syria for *Charisma News*:

> The army of Assad is wiping out city after city—both the Islamic rebels and Assad's army kill everybody in their way—and the victims are mostly found among the innocent: children, women who have been raped, people murdered in front of their family, old people who are tortured. For millions of people, hell has arrived in their land. Over 3 million refugees have fled Syria, 1.5 million of which escaped to Jordan. (*Hell Has Arrived in Syria*, 5/23/2014, www.charismanews.com/opinion/43959-hell-has-arrived-in-syria)

The Muslim fighters are also enforcing Sharia Law to the point that <u>they are even making the Christian towns submit to them or be killed</u>, and the Christians are submitting. Pray for them, and support Christian ministries that help persecuted Christians, such as *Voice of the Martyrs* and *Samaritan's Purse*.

The Arab Spring has transitioned into a war to bring back the Islamic caliphate, and the empire. So we are very close to the start of the final years of the Gospel Age, and the Great Trib.

Now that you have read this book I hope you can see how far off the idea of a European one-world government is. I hope you can you see how ridiculous it is to believe that Muslims, who are brainwashed from birth, will forsake it all to follow some European world leader who claims to be God. Nonsense. How could he be more evil than Islam? Islam is not a mere religion, it is a totalitarian system out to rule the world at any cost, and it is the religion of Satan. It has been called a death cult. We don't need to look for a European leader to deceive people into following him into tyranny. It has already happened. Islam is the mother of all nightmare religious cults.

Some people do not like people pointing out the evils of Islam, and want to point out that Christianity has also killed people in war and persecution. If all that Islam did was only in the past, then what they did would merely be part of history. But Muslims are still wanting to conquer the world, and they are still teaching it in their mosques and schools, and they are still acting in the same way as they did in history by killing Christians and Jews. But Christianity is not still warring against people or persecuting them. The reason for this difference is that killing to spread the religion is part of the Islamic faith, but it is not actually part of the Christian faith.

Also, if you look at how many were killed by Christian wars and persecution, and how many have been killed by Islam, the numbers are very lopsided. Christians killed a few million; Muslims killed a few *hundred million.*

Another accusation could be that I am only focusing on the negative elements of Islam. I am sure that good things could be said about the Roman Empire or even Hitler, but that would not remove the evil of that they did. If you don't want to believe that normal everyday Islam wants to wage WW3, here it is in their own words written by a Member of the Supreme Council for Islamic Media, and Prof. of 'Aqeedah and Contemporary Religions and Madhhabs, at King Sa'ood University, Riyadh, Saudi Arabia:

> Sometimes you hear about the appearance of the Mahdi, sometimes you hear that the time for the <u>final major battle against the Jews and Christians</u> is close at hand, other times you hear about landslides in the East or in the West, and so forth.
>
> . . . we should act in accordance with what Islam has enjoined in general, which is to support the religion of Islam, defend Muslim lands, <u>establish Jihad for the sake of Allah</u>, and <u>fight</u> to raise the banner of Islam.
>
> The Muslims today must prepare to <u>fight the Jews and expel the Christians</u> who are occupying Muslim lands, and not sit idle in humiliation, waiting for the Mahdi to emerge to save us. Rather we should unite and support our religion, and if the Mahdi ap-

pears we will support him. (*The End of the World: The Major and Minor Signs of the Hour*, by Dr. Muhammad al-'Areefi. Darussalam, New York, 2008.(page 17, 257)

The above mentioned book was published by one of the largest Islamic publishing houses in the world that have offices in Riyadh, Jeddah, Sharjah, Lahore, London, New York, and Houston.

The latest news is that ISIS is almost defeated in Syria and Iraq, but experts say it will be nearly impossible to totally defeat them because there are so many caves in a vast area for them to hide. But even if they were to be totally defeated, that will not stop the other groups who are actively working to bring back the caliphate, which includes Turkey.

Now that you have a broad view of what is happening in Turkey and the Middle East, and how Bible prophecy refers to Islam and Muhammad, you can see how the beast is even now rising from the Abyss: Turkey will say that the only way to stabilize the Muslim nations that have fallen into turmoil is to put them all back under Turkey's rule. And you see how even Western nations could agree, and say, yes, you can take control of those nations to stop the flow of refugees flooding into Europe and even North America. That would seem to be a logical answer to the problem, and fulfillment of Bible prophecy!

But if it happens that way, it will not be the start of the 42 months. In BK1 I originally had the beast existing for only 42 months, but it is possible that it will revive its empire, then later it will call for jihad, which would then begin the final 42 months. Or, the 42 months could begin once there are a total of 10 nations that are part of the empire. It is impossible to know all the details in advance, so we should keep watching, because we are in the last years and there is NO pretribulation Rapture, it is closer to Mid-Trib than Post-Trib, (see BK1 for more info on the Rapture). (It was until mid 2020 pre-Wrath yet Post-Trib, but that was a mistake I have now changed to near Mid-Trib; I am calling it Mid-Trib though I don't believe in the traditional 7-year period; see BK1 for more details.)

Tell everyone you know about this book because it has little to no advertising budget. Post on Facebook, Twitter, blogs, Youtube, and write a review for me online. Be sure to visit my website, www.usbibleprophecy.com for updates to this book and info on other books.

Should it ever become illegal to criticize Islam in the U.S., this book will be forced to go out of print, but at that time you can copy and share the eBook edition of this book for as long as it is illegal or make photocopies. If you live now in a country where it is illegal to criticize Islam, you are free to share the eBook edition of this book in that nation at no cost.

Last of all, there are wannabe prophets on youtube and TV saying that the pope is the false prophet of Revelation 13. I have already presented much proof against that view. Pope Francis is pushing Chrislam because he is trying to bring peace. Chrislam is not a good thing, but it is not the death cult of Islam. He is pushing it because he hopes to change the prophecies that say the last pope will be killed, and he knows he is the last pope! (see Book 1 for more on the last pope)

Bible Prophecy Revealed
Book 1
Discoveries in Bible Prophecy

Book 2
The Beast and False Prophet Revealed

Book 3
The Fall of Babylon the Great America

Book 4
The Approaching Apocalypse and Three Days of Darkness

Editing God: Textual Criticism and Modern Bibles Analyzed.
Satan's False Prophets Exposed.

Selected Bibliography

Al-Khairiyyah, Mussasat Al-Haramain. *Saad bin Abi Waqqas*. Riyadh, Saudi Abrabia: Alharamain Islamic Foundation, 1999.

Al-Shinnawy, Abdul Aziz. *The Islamic Openings*. Al-Mansura, Egypt: Umm Al-Qura, 2002.

Ali, Maulana Muhammad. *The Religion of Islam*. Ahmadiyyah Anjuman Ishaat Islam Lahore: Columbus, OH, 1990.

Ali, Maulana Muhammad. *Holy Quran: English Translation and Commentary*. Ahmadiyyah Anjuman Ishaat Islam Lahore: Columbus, OH, 1994.

Ali, Ahmed. *Sacred Writings, Islam: The Quran*. Quality Paperback Book Club, New York, 1992.

Ali, Syed Amir. *A Short History of the Saracens: Being a Concise Account of the Rise and Decline of the Saracenic Power*. First published in 1926; this edition published in New Delhi, India: Kitab Bhavan, 1994.

Ayoub, Sami and Vivian Ayoub. *Men in Captivity*. New York: Darussalam, 2002.

Barclay, William. *The Revelation of John*, Vol. 1. Louisville, KY. Westminster John Knox Press, 1976, 2004.

Barclay, William. *The Revelation of John*, Vol. 2, revised edition. Philadelphia: Westminster Press, 1976.

Bellock, Hilaire. *The Battle Ground: Syria and Palestine: The Seedplot of Religion*. San Francisco: Ignatius Press , 2008.

Bovard, James. *Terrorism and Tyranny: Trampling Freedom, Justice, and Peace to Rid the World of Evil*. New York: St. Martin's Press, 2003.

Butler, Alfred. *The Arab Invasion of Egypt, and the Last 30 Years of the Roman Dominion*; 1902. Republished by A & B Publishing Group, Brooklyn, New York: 1992.

Clifton, Tony and Rod Nordland. *"The Islamic Nightmare."* Newsweek, 14 October 1996.

Crawford, Paul F. *"Four Myths about the Crusades."* First Principles Journal. April 21, 2011. (www.firstprinciplesjournal.com/ articles.aspx?loc=ja&article=1483)

Croutier, Alev Lytle. *Harem: The World Behind the Veil*. Abbeville Press: New York, 1989.

Davis, Joyce M. *Between Jihad and Salaam: Profiles in Islam*. New York: St. Martin's Press, 1997.

Dinet, Etienne and Sliman Ben Ibrahim. *The Life of Mohammad: The Prophet of Allah*. Secacus, NJ: Chartwell Books, 1990.

Earle, Ralph. *Word Meanings in the New Testament*. Grand Rapids: Baker Book House, 1986.

Emmett, Chad F. *Beyond the Bascilica: Christians and Muslims in Nazareth*. Chicago: Univ. of Chicago Press, 1995.

Erikson, Marc. *"Islamism, Fascism and Terrorism."* Asia Times, Nov 5, 2002. (www. atimes.com /atimes /Middle_East/DK05Ak01.html)

Foxe, John. Rewritten and updated by Harold J. Chadwick. *The New Foxe's Book of Martyrs*. North Brunswick, NJ: Bridge-Logos Publishers, 1997.

Gabriel, Mark A. *Islam and Terrorism*. Lake Mary, FL: Charisma House, 2002.

Gibbon, Edward. *The Decline And Fall Of The Roman Empire*.

Green, Jay P. General Editor and translator. *The Interlinear Greek-English New Testament*. Peabody, MA: Hendrickson Publishers, 1985.

Hailey, Homer. *Revelation: An Introduction and Commentary*. Grand Rapids: Baker Book House, 1979.

Halley, Henry H. *Halley's Bible Handbook*. 24th ed. Grand Rapids: Zondervan, 1965.

Hendrikson, W. *More Than Conquerors*. Grand Rapids: Baker Book House, 1940.

Huband, Mark. *Warriors of the Prophet: The Struggle for Islam*. Boulder, CO: Westview Press, 1998.

Kaiser, Walter C. Jr. *Back Toward the Future: Hints for Interpreting Biblical Prophecy*. Grand Rapids: Baker Book House, 1989.

Khan, Muqtedar. *"A Fresh look at Sayyid Qutb's Milestones."* The Milli Gazette, 2000. (www.milligazette.com/Archives/01-8-2000/art4.htm) Krauthammer, Charles. *"A Desecration of the Truth."* Time, 14 October 1996.

Lari, Sayid Mujtaba Rukni Musawi. *Western Civilisation Through Muslim Eyes*. Houston: Free Islamic Literature, Inc., 1974.

Laurence, Richard. *The Book of Enoch Updated*. Edited by Michael D. Fortner. Lawton, Ok: Trumpet Press, 2012.

Leiner, Frederick C. *The End of Barbary Terror: America's 1815 War Against the Pirates of North Africa*. Oxford U. Press, 2007.
Nicolle, David. *Yarmuk AD 636: The Muslim conquest of Syria*. Osprey Publishing, 1994.

Palmer, Andrew, Sebastian P. Brock, Robert Hoyland. *The Seventh Century in the West-Syrian Chronicles*. Liverpool: Liverpool University Press, 1993.

Payne, Robert. *The History of Islam*. New York: Dorset, 1959.

Peters, F.E. *The Hajj: The Muslim Pilgrimage to Mecca and The Holy Places*. Princeton: Princeton University Press, 1994.

Ross Jr., Frank. *Arabs and the Islamic World*. New York: S.G. Phillips, 1979.

Runciman, Steven. *The Fall of Constantinople 1453*. Cambridge: Cambridge Univ. Press, 1965.

Richardson, Joel. *The Islamic Antichrist*. Los Angeles: WND Books, 2009.

Sabini, John. *Islam: A Primer*. Washington, D.C.: Middle East Editorial Associates, 1983.

Scally, John. *100 Irish Rugby Greats.* Edinburgh, Scotland: Mainstream Publishing Company. 2011.

Sheen, Bishop Fulton J. *World's First Love,* Ignatius Press, San Francisco, 1996.

Shoebat, Walid, and Joel Richardson. *God's War on Terror*. Top Executive Media, 2008.

Spencer, Robert. *The Politically Incorrect Guide to Islam and the Crusades*. Washington, DC: Regnery Publishing, 2005.

Stewart, Desmon. *Early Islam*. New York: Time Incorporated, 1967.

Stone, Jr., Perry. *Unleashing the Beast*. Cleveland: Voice of Evangelism, 2003.

Suermann, Prof. Dr. Harald. *Copts and the Islam of the Seventh Century.* Published in, Christian-Muslim Relations; A Bibliographical History, Volume 5. David Thomas.

The Noble Quran, In The English Language, Summariized on One Volume, by Dr. Muhammad Muhsin Khan, Dr. Muhammad Taqi-ud -Din Al-Hilali, Alharamain Islamic Foundation, Islamic Foundation Center of America, Ashland, OR, 1996.

Tolan , John Victor, editor. *Medieval Christian Perceptions of Islam.* New York: Routledge, 1996.

Trifkovic, Serge. *The Sword of the Prophet.* Boston: Regina Orthodox Press, 2002.

Vester, Bertha Spafford. *Our Jerusalem: An American Family in the Holy City, 1881-1949.* Garden City, NY: Doubleday, 1950.

Walden, Andrew. *Thomas Jefferson, Ben Franklin, John Adams and James Madison: Young America's Fight with Islamism.* 15 Jan. 2007. www.islam-watch.org/ThomasJefferson/Founding_Fathers_ Fight_Islam. Htm

Williams, John Alden, editor. *Islam.* George Braziller: New York, 1961.

Zakaria, Fareed. *"Why Do They Hate Us?"* Newsweeks, 15, October 2001

Zodhiates, Spiros. *The Complete Word Study Dictionary: New Testament.* Chattanooga, TN: AMG Publishers, 1992.

Zondervan NIV Bible Commentary. Vol. 1 & 2. Grand Rapids: Zondervan Publishing House, 1994.

Manufactured by Amazon.ca
Bolton, ON

19485132R00113